PENELOPE

The World of Each Other

Paul Bochner

PENELOPE: THE WORLD OF EACH OTHER

Copyright © 2025 by Paul Bochner

Published by Compass Rose Publishing
228 Park Ave. S #620056 New York, NY. 10003-1502

Printed in the United States of America

Hardcover ISBN# 979-8-9988995-2-2

Softcover ISBN# 979-8-9988995-1-5

No part of this publication may be reproduced, distributed, or transmitted in any form or by any means, including photocopying, recording, or other electronic or mechanical methods, without the publisher's prior written permission, except as permitted by U.S. copyright law.

PHOTO CREDIT
All photos by author except as noted:
Page 29: Barbara Labrake
Page 68: David Ross
Page 187 and 222: Joel Carreiro
Author photo: Cornelia Elizabeth Bochner

Cover and Interior Design by Madeline Mafilios and Thomas Hurd.

First Edition

All rights reserved

For Connie, most exquisite

Contents

2014

The world of each other   2

2015

You are not alone   10

The nature of love   36

Crossing the threshold   47

Abandonment   52

On our own   55

Standing up for her   57

Clarity   60

Opening to her   63

Eugenics   66

Things happen   70

Vulnerability   73

As new life begins   85

Uncertainty   87

Human / Animal   94

Contents

2016

Hollywood meets Penelope	118
Home to many	121
Time	148
Penelope has given birth	158
The coyote in daylight	173
Detachment and attachment	175

2017

Fully alive	210
An exceptional day	214
When it pivots	232
Eclipse	258

2019

Postscript	268

2025

Acknowledgments	274

At sunset, after the rain, Penelope came back. We stood in the last light, bright and cool, igniting each auburn hair along her neck and back, illuminating her translucent ears. Longing for the light to fade and take away the burden of more beauty than I could bear, I fed her strawberries, black grapes, fed her extravagantly, as much as she wanted, for every reason. This was her triumph, to be celebrated. We had lived through pain, fear, and uncertainty, the risings in the dark, endured the winter and the cold, all of it leading us here, a June day of survival, and I silently thought, "This is your prize, your literal moment in the sun. We have every richness, and it is all for you."

The world of each other

Emerging gently from forests in the half-light of dawn, vanishing silently, appearing again at dusk, deer seem to reside in a parallel plane. Nearly illusory in their graceful presence, so masterfully camouflaged that they can be invisible when they are in front of us, their passage on the Earth is brief. They rarely interact with humans.

Yet one remarkable fawn arose from the dream world. The first time we saw each other, in early June, 2014, she was a day or two old, poised in sunlight under tall pines in an area I regard as the deer sanctuary, half an acre of wooded land in front of my home. I leave it untouched for them, effectively a continuation of the many protected acres of trees, stream, and pond on the other side of the road, their natural habitat, and each spring the deer give birth here.

On that morning, I stood a few yards from the fawn, certain that her mother was nearby and protectively watching. I admired the fresh sienna coat with its scattering of white spots, her dark eyes and slender, long legs, and I took her photograph, which I sent to a friend with the words "perfect new life." The new life

may have been perfect in the moment, but it would not remain so. When I saw her a few weeks later, the fawn's left forelimb was broken, her foot turned under, facing backward rather than forward, her weight borne by her wrist. With each halting and tender step, her injured leg collapsed. More significantly, her mother had abandoned her and she was solitary.

The disabled fawn then vanished. I thought of her from time to time, assuming she had perished. I could not have guessed that she would eventually reappear. I could never have imagined how she would alter the ways in which I see the world. Over the next several years a sequence of events would lead us across boundaries widely thought to be unbridgeable.

It might seem improbable that, living only nineteen miles from New York City, I could develop and sustain a relationship with a wild deer, yet such a connection would be improbable anywhere, given a deer's innate wariness. Having lived in their presence for decades, I had paid as much attention to deer as I paid to squirrels, which is to say not much. Yet I had observed them enough to learn that a whitetail fawn enjoys a strong bond with its mother, continuing to nurse for several months, well past the time it begins eating vegetation, staying close to its family for protection and guidance. A female may remain with its mother for life, a male for at least its first year, and what we term a herd is generally a matriarchal family of several generations. They forage together, sleep in a cluster, play games at dusk, running, leaping, chasing each other, and the young are well protected. A disabled fawn, isolated, unable to run or even to properly walk, is likely to be targeted by a coyote, a fox, or a large raptor, swift death all but certain.

In that June week, three fawns had been born to two mothers, or so it had appeared to me. Following the disappearance of the disabled fawn, the remaining twins and their mother stayed in the deer sanctuary throughout the summer and fall. The abandoning doe, seeming to have driven away her unwanted offspring, was herself gone. The twins and their mother settled into the sanctuary, sleeping under the pines, eating plentiful greenery, wandering only short distances. This stretch of land, safely above the road, provides shelter, and with its range of vegetation to eat and nest in, with fresh water nearby, they had all they needed.

As autumn gave way to the extremely hard winter of 2015, with record cold temperatures, strong winds, ice, and massive snowfall, the deer grew their characteristic grey-brown, thick, and shaggy winter coats, resembling donkey fur, in contrast to their sleek summer coats. In winter, under normal circumstances, deer subsist on the twigs, dead leaves, evergreen needles, and small branches left exposed. With deep snow on the ground there seemed almost nothing available, and I began tossing pieces of apple and bread for them. On nights when the temperature, with wind chill, would fall to twenty degrees below zero Fahrenheit, the three would be at the door at ten thirty, often back again at four in the morning, back at eight and so through the day.

After their late evening feeding, they would go around to their sanctuary in front of the house and settle into nests in the snow, depressions of customized size, carved out with their front feet. Lying close to each other, their body heat melting the snow, they sank within it to a floor of leaves. Moving and living as a unit, rarely more than a few feet from one another, the twins had the advantage of being together under their mother's care and protection, and of receiving supplemental nutrition from me. Because of the harsh conditions, I found myself paying attention to the deer for the first time, becoming invested in their well-being.

I had assumed the abandoned fawn had died, but I was wrong. I occasionally caught fleeting glimpses of her, at a distance, always alone, sometimes barely able to move, and I could not imagine how she was surviving. Almost certainly keeping to herself in the woods across the road, where she may have found a sheltered nesting spot beside the stream, eating what was within reach, spending her days and nights lying still, she may have been waiting in vain for her mother to return to her, to take her back, waiting for healing which would never come. I had begun to think of her as The Girl with the Broken Foot.

It is hard to witness any life in pain, harder to contemplate a young creature left to die, particularly so when the new life is a graceful mammal with large eyes and soft coloration, attributes which inspire our adoration and nurturance. It is challenging to construct the intention of an abandoning mother. Freeing herself and her healthy fawns of the burden of a disabled family member, which would slow them in their foraging, and perhaps attract predators, obeying an evolutionary imperative to nurture only the healthiest offspring, a mother might anticipate that a rejected fawn, deprived of a mother's nursing, guidance, and protection, would quickly perish.

2015

You are
not alone

On the evening of March 18, as it was growing dark, I went to the window, not knowing what was drawing me. Next to the house stood a shadow, ghost-like, shrunken, at one with the dusk, almost translucent, and I recognized The Girl with the Broken Foot.

I walked out into the wet falling snow, slowly approaching her, and she allowed me to come close. Nine months old, she was the size of a fawn half that age. Starkly emaciated, her body seemed to be collapsing inward, her head held low. Literal hunger and a deeper starvation were palpable. She bore the haunted look of terminal solitude seen in souls driven to the margins of society, among the living, yet apart. She seemed so frail that I couldn't imagine she would live more than another day or two.

Going in and returning with a bowl of apples, I began to cut them into pieces and placed a few on the ground between us. She was ravenously hungry and I gave her a few more apples, and still more, until she had eaten a total of eight. After she had finished eating, she stayed with me. We stood about a foot apart. She showed no fear

Penelope

of me, a fact which I would later come to recognize as meaningful. The moment had the compelling quality which has been present at the onset of many enduring connections in my life, of being unbound by linear time.

"I am watching over you," I said softly. "If you come here, I will take care of you. You are not alone."

It was fully dark when we parted, having been together for an hour. I expected that she would recede into the woods, yet the next morning she was sleeping against the house, directly beneath the window closest to where I sit all day to work. Save for the wall separating us, she could not have gotten any closer to me.

When I went around to the front of the house, she struggled to her feet and approached. In the morning light, I was better able to assess the state of her health. Months of solitary survival had taken a severe toll. Her body seemed hollowed, her ribs and pelvis

sharply visible beneath her skin, and it felt a miracle that she was alive. On her right flank was a hemispherical mass the size of a cantaloupe, which I took to be a tumor, yet it had an open, running wound at its center, which she periodically craned her neck to lick. Her eyes were running and had congealed masses at their inner corners.

I bent to get a look at her injured foot. From not being walked on, the backward-facing cloven hoof had grown to an abnormal length and was curling upwards. The wrist, which unnaturally bore her weight, had a flattened forward surface, an oval about two inches across, worn raw, without hair or skin, only pale pink-grey flesh which at its center appeared to have been further abraded to the bone. Her right front foot, forced to compensate, was splayed and rockered, her right scapular protruded and her front quarters were substantially lower than her hips.

I again placed apple pieces on the ground between us. I spoke very gently to her, saying "You are the best one of all the deer. You are the most beautiful. You are good." I continued to talk to her while she ate her apples, and when she had taken all she could she returned to her resting spot under the window. I went inside to work, keeping periodic watch, pleased that she seemed to have claimed a place. But in a few minutes, from around the corner of the house came the twins, followed by their mother who immediately and aggressively charged at her. The Girl with the Broken Foot lurched upright and hobbled down the embankment, across the road and into the woods.

She was once again alone, but a step had been taken. Since the previous evening, things had changed. Even before her second feeding she had recognized me on sight. She had approached and had again allowed me near.

Although I had seen her fewer than half a dozen times in the preceding months, from the night of our first connection she began to come to the house every day. She slowly gained strength and I would watch for her and thrill to the sight of her slow approach. It was our private time. We stood together, and I placed her food on the ground between us. After she ate, she would stare into my eyes for long periods, seemingly entranced. I told her stories. I sang softly to her. I told her she was my beauty.

So began our journey, and one of the greatest loves I have ever known.

It took courage for the fawn to make her way to the property, never knowing whether she would be harshly chased by the other deer, yet she came. In our hours together, wanting to share her experience of the moment, I gave myself no comfort or protection that she did not have, standing in the cold and rain with her, without jacket or boots, as on our first night. Day by day she learned to rely on my being here. I fed her and I offered the sound of my voice, which she seemed to

Penelope

enjoy, telling her that she had been made special for a reason, even if we couldn't know yet what the reason was. I told her that some suffer more than others and that suffering often confers gifts.

As spring advanced, her aspect and demeanor shifted, her facial expression and posture conveying a quality I can only term pride. She stood in front of me and held her injured foot above the ground as if asking that I acknowledge her wound. She seemed to know that, after a life alone, she had attained a form of recognition and now had someone of her own.

By fortunate circumstance, I worked at home and was at that time living alone, without commitments to wife or family, and had one quietly aging dog, who stayed largely indoors, enabling me to be almost continuously present, open to what might come.

As the Girl with the Broken Foot became part of my daily life, several friends asked if I had named her. I was adamant about not doing so; to name her was to court attachment, and a tide of human losses, too much heartache, had washed me to the present shore. Loss is often close at hand and, given time, loss is assured. I would not be able to protect her, or so it reasonably seemed, couldn't bring the disabled fawn inside, could not take her to the veterinarians for corrective surgery. She might perish from the cold, be struck by a car or attacked by a coyote. While I might in time arrive at a moment of grief over the loss of this deer, the grief would be lessened if she did not have a name.

Yet a name was in me. I had silently begun to think of her as Penelope.

One day I spoke it. She began gradually to respond, and once she had a name, our connection deepened, enlarging my feelings toward her. Initially, Penelope had secret places in the woods where she spent her nights, perhaps the same places where she had hidden and survived alone when very young, trying to heal after her abandonment. She regularly appeared at the house before sunrise, sometimes while it was still dark. As the days grew long, I was sure to get up at four fifteen in order to be outside, waiting. I would scan for any small sign

I had silently begun to think of her as Penelope.

of her. At her approach I was filled with joyful relief to know that she had survived another night. When aggressive deer tried to chase her, I stood with her and protected her, making it clear that the property was her haven.

During many weeks of daily feeding, Penelope became markedly healthier and stronger. Eye contact, the sound of a gentle voice, the offering of good food, all may have contributed toward recovery in ways we often intuit but cannot define. The open wound on her flank healed, the mass beneath it vanished. On the damaged leg, flesh and skin grew over her raw and flattened wrist and formed a kind of callus, allowing her to walk on it more freely, although still with difficulty, and some days with evident pain. She seemed to be organically healthier as well. I believe that there is life-enhancing power in love, and I was seeing it happen.

JUNE 4

Penelope lives wild and free, she comes and goes as she wishes, and is usually outside each morning as soon as the sky begins to glow. In the quiet stillness, she and I stand in the first half-light. I feed her, then she stands in front of me and grooms herself, showing me her left side, her right, her legs, her tail. As we share these moments, without another deer or person in sight, an extraordinary peace enfolds us. I talk quietly to her and tell her how good she is, that she is becoming more beautiful by the day. I say that she is looking strong and that her summer coat is such a remarkable color, luminous and lush, the deepest and most golden of any of the deer.

After going off to spend her day in the woods and along the lake, she appears again before sunset. Her broken foot is still broken of course—some days it appears to cause her more pain than others—yet I now see it as a sign of distinction which renders her singular and even more beautiful. It is her challenge, and challenges can become sources of strength. She and I have our own language of words and phrases, hand signals, bodily gestures, and postures. Our communication is precise and we have developed it together, she teaching me as I have taught her. She controls our relationship. I place her needs first and respect her pace. We have good times, and whatever our notional distinctions, neither of us seems to care.

Initially, there was much I could not know about the solitary fawn, and assumptions which, through surmise and incomplete observation, I would get wrong. Only after months of studying her and the other deer in the vicinity did I begin to gain fuller understanding of her situation. The more I learned about this individual deer, the greater my admiration and respect for deer as a species. They live gently and lightly upon the earth. As herbivores, they take only what they need, causing no pain or death.

Whitetail deer in this part of the country do not stray far from where they are born. With a potential life span of about ten years, which is generally reduced to four and a half years in the wild, females in particular live in a carefully prescribed area known as their range, in this case an area about a third of a mile long by several hundred yards wide, bounded on the east by the protected woods and fresh stream, and on the west by the five-mile-long lake, itself surrounded by protected woodland, supporting a profusion of wildlife. With fewer than a dozen houses in the range, almost none of them fenced, the deer move freely through many wooded acres and browse among lawns, some gently tended, others open and semi-wild. The environment provides the deer with space to roam and to rest, two sources of fresh water, and plenty to eat in the warmer months.

Each spring, from mid-May into early June, the females come to the sanctuary in front of the house to deliver their fawns, usually in one very precise area no larger than a breakfast table. I wonder whether this small spot may have been a focal birthing point for thousands of years, such are the mysteries of their connection to the earth. At two years of age, a doe will give birth to her first single fawn, and in subsequent years will usually deliver twins or triplets. A fawn can rise to its feet and walk within twenty minutes of being born, and having tested its legs, taking a few unsteady steps, it obeys the mother's instruction, communicated with the lightest touch of her muzzle, to remain hidden and be utterly still. The doe hides each newborn for about twelve days, placing it securely in a high growth of shrubbery or flowers, or within a pile of branches and twigs, all of which I leave undisturbed for that purpose.

Infrequently, a doe will hide her fawn in a man-made area that feels semi-enclosed, anywhere the fawn is likely to avoid visual detection by a predator. A fawn has no scent, but its mother does, and for this reason she doesn't stay with the baby during her daytime hours, spending them apart but not too distant from the fawn, leaving it before first light and returning several times to nurse. If she has had a multiple birth, she will hide each of her fawns in its own spot, well separated from the others, sometimes by hundreds of feet, within her established range. In this way, should a coyote or fox appear, it might take only a single offspring. The fawns lie still for periods of up to sixteen hours, awaiting their mother's return.

Hidden fawns are not always completely invisible. Over the years I have found them in an array of semi-camouflage—in a patch of irises, in compost piles, within a stack of twigs, in a corner of the house between a wall and staircase. Some mothers are better than others at hiding and I have seen more than one fawn "hidden" openly at the base of a tree. One year a fawn was hidden in the middle of the lawn.

Someone finding a fawn and not knowing the protocol of its concealment may think the baby has been abandoned. The mother knows where her fawn is and will return for it at dusk. Because a doe with triplets will hide each of them in a separate place for the first many days of their lives, reuniting them only in the dark, it can initially be hard to know how many births have occurred to one doe. When they are about two weeks old, the fawns are released from their hiding places by their mother's silent signal and from that point they spend day and night together, inseparable, moving as a family.

Most cervine mothers are fiercely protective, cleaning and nursing their fawns, rushing to them when they call. A fawn seeks proximity to its family, physically reconnecting after any separation by mutual nuzzling and licking, resuming their places side by side. They are delicate yet strong, and an adult whitetail—so named for the brilliant white underside of the tail, held erect when there is danger—can run forty miles an hour and jump an eight-foot wall. To observe a young fawn in springtime, to see it running and twisting, exploring its range of motion, its capacity for speed and for leaping, is to feel a shared elation.

August 2015

Since early spring, Penelope has come each day, usually twice, and we enjoy a serene understanding that when she appears, I will devote myself to her, feeding her and communicating in a variety of ways. Our shared hours have developed a sense of commitment, and we spend substantial time simply being together. From the first, I had placed Penelope's sliced apple pieces on the ground between us, a few inches from my foot, where she showed me she wanted them. As she bent to pick them up, I could easily have reached out to touch her, but I was careful to never violate her sense of safety and comfort, even accidentally. On some days, I would extend a piece of apple in my fingers, toward her mouth. She would lean backwards, keeping her front feet in place but moving her face away, telling me that taking food from the ground and taking it from my hand were not the same, that she didn't yet trust me well enough. I would then gently place the apple on the ground, to show her that I understood, that I did not need her to eat from my fingers, that it wasn't an issue, there was no cause to worry.

Once or twice, as I extended the apple slice, she placed her lips on it before withdrawing, leaving the piece in my fingers. But by early August there were small signs that she was preparing to take it. I could tell by her expression as I held an apple piece toward her, as she hesitated a tiny bit, as if to indicate that it might not be too bad, that it might even be nice, that she was thinking about it.

On Thursday August 6, her approach and hesitation were different. I extended my hand. We each understood that this was something we hadn't done, that we might need to just get over it, and that she was the one who had to be ready. She quickly reached for the piece of apple, took it in her lips, chewed, and swallowed. Then she abruptly backed off and snorted, a strong exhalation of relieved stress, as when we try something we have feared and realize that not only have we done it, but nothing terrible has happened in consequence.

She took only one piece from my hand that morning. I placed the following pieces on the ground, not wishing to force anything. But the line had been crossed. The next day, she wanted to eat every bite from my hands, as she did the two following days.

Penelope

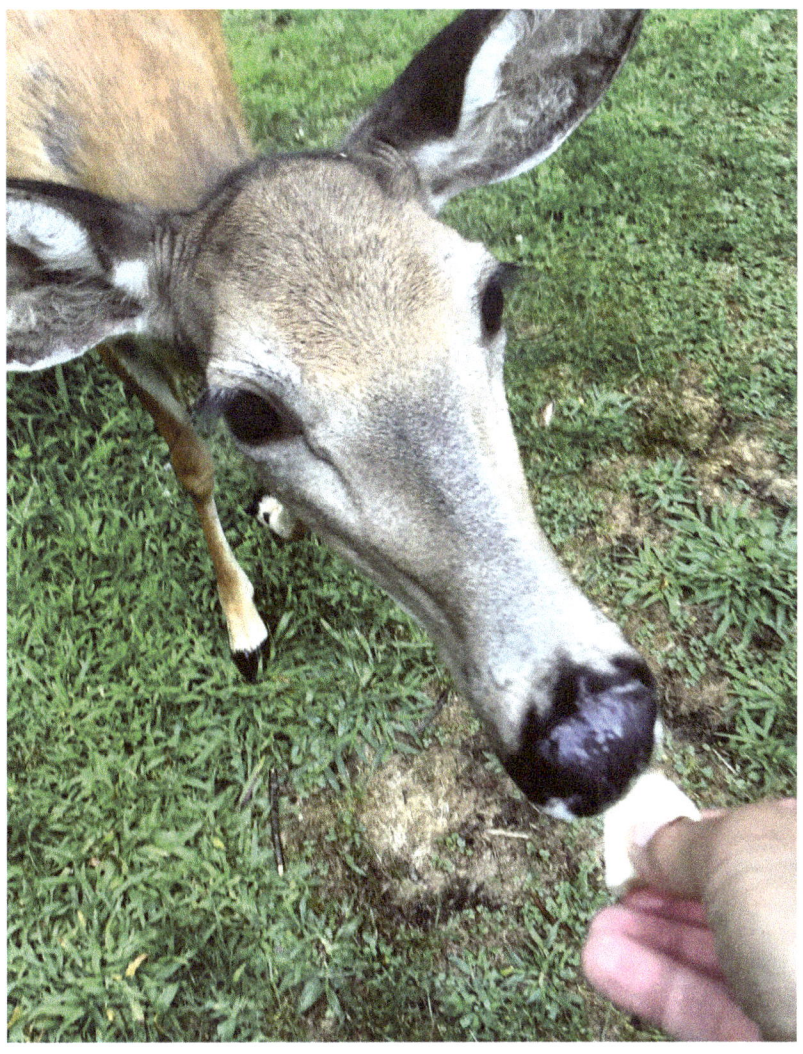

Sunday, August 9, light rain was falling. I saw her standing under the small red maple. I went and stood with her, in a sublime moment, as the shelter of a tree and gossamer summer rain will provide. I had an apple, which I cut and fed to her. She ate from my fingers. Then, for the first time, she licked my hands at length. This gesture carried greater meaning than the taking of food. She was grooming me as deer groom each other, particularly between mothers and fawns. A day or two later she began licking not only my hands but my wrists and forearms. As she licked me, I stroked her muzzle. She seemed starved

Paul Bochner

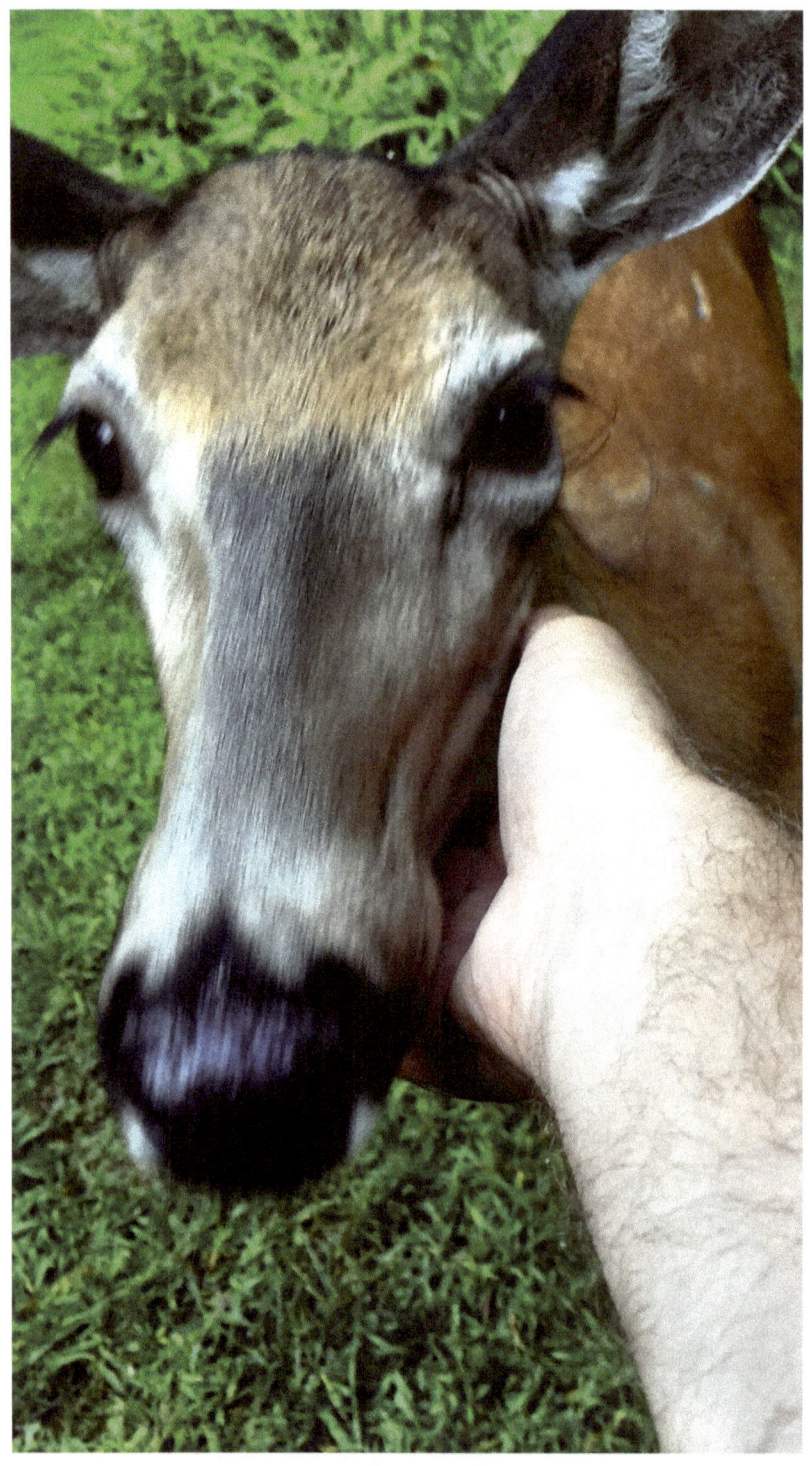

Penelope

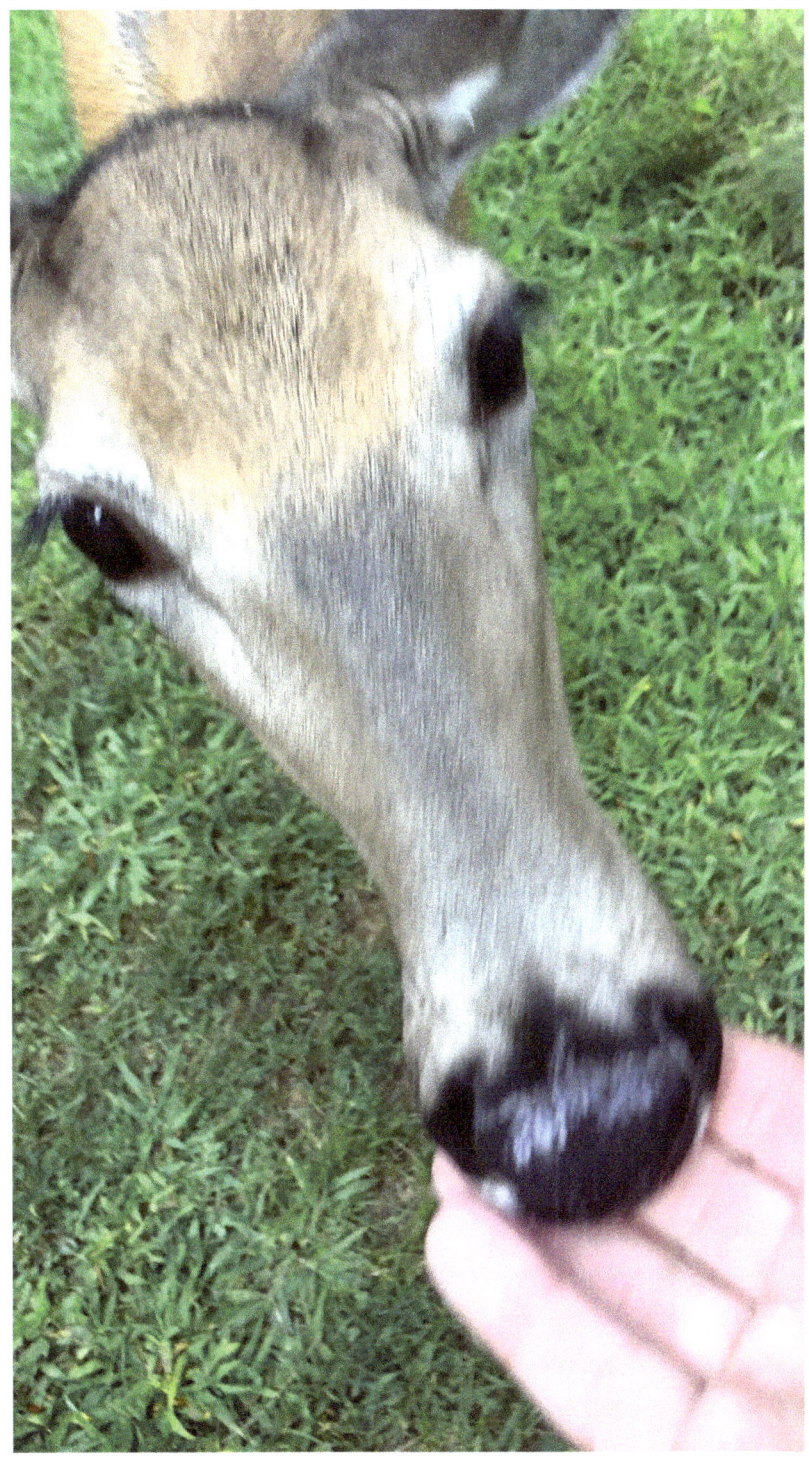

for touch and let me stroke her neck, under her chin, the sides of her face, visibly luxuriating in the feel of my hand.

Beginning with our initial one-on-one contact, from the first night I fed her and spoke to her, in four months she had accepted me.

Among all that Penelope has been denied by her mother's rejection, grooming has been a primal deprivation. A doe will lick her offspring for long periods, far longer than the dictates of cleaning require, and at the same time a fawn will reciprocate. There is evident rapture for both. Not having had the physical connection, Penelope now seemed to realize that she could have it with me. The nature of our touching progressed in stages, as it does between people. Some weeks after her stroking and licking were established as part of our daily routine, she very tentatively touched my torso with her nose, all but imperceptibly, just once. The next day she did it again, a bit more clearly. Within days she began pressing her face into my chest and abdomen, rubbing her muzzle between my arm and body.

Each day, Penelope touches me and invites me to touch her. She seems not to mind that we are of different species, an erasure that supports my sense that boundaries are for crossing, and that once they are dissolved, true connection is possible. Face to face with her, without effort, I remove the things which separate us, let go of my identity as a human, do not regard her as a deer so much as simply another living creature.

Having lived in proximity to deer for many years, having watched them grazing at dusk, having seen them lying dead by the edge of the road, I had never known one as an individual. In ways I could not have imagined, Penelope is complex and subtle. She has a broad range of expression and emotion, a sense of humor and a sense of play. I know when she is having a hard day, when she is exhausted, when she is in physical pain. Conversely, I can sometimes see that she is feeling well, during an hour or a day free from pain. She loses patience with me, snorting if I don't do what she expects and I make sure she is the one to establish the rules. She comes to me as she wishes, and I try to be there, waiting. Whenever she is ready, she turns and hobbles back into the woods and to her natural life. Our connection is based on her needs and wants. If we were two people, such an imbalance would be unhealthy, but here it is right.

In this area of several square miles, inhabited by thousands of people and hundreds of deer, there is, as far as I know, one such bond between one deer and one person. If there were another, I would have heard about it. From my first sighting of her following her injury and abandonment, my compassion and empathy were engaged. I wanted the fawn with the broken foot to survive. I gradually wanted to be able to protect her and to nourish her. That much of this has come about, not through my actions but through hers, feels wondrous to me. At the writing of this passage, in August of 2015, Penelope is fourteen months old. She lives freely, moving about her range, finding flowers, leaves, and grasses to eat, sleeping in the woods, drinking from the lake or stream. Each morning, upon waking, she makes her way to me. I rise at four fifteen so that I will be outside to greet her. I sit with coffee, the newspaper, her wooden bowl holding a dozen apples.

I scan the wooded areas and the high-grown, meadow-like property next door for the first sign of her. Penelope and I sometimes see each other from a distance. Even in semi-darkness, I know her unique rising and falling motion as she walks, akin to the walk of a person with one leg several inches shorter than the other, and as I watch her movements it is evident that the journey to see me costs substantial effort and pain. My anxiety that something may have happened to her in the night is reasonable, and my relief at first sight is wonderful. I feel a surge of joy, knowing that she has survived the night, that she is coming to me and we will begin our morning. To let her know that in a sense we are meeting halfway, I walk a few yards in her direction and speak her name quietly. She moves toward me haltingly but directly, with intention. There are times when, absorbed in the paper, I will have missed her silent approach. I glance up to find her standing a few feet away, sometimes still half asleep, with bits of vegetation woven in her coat, looking at me. She yawns, and sometimes her yawn makes me yawn, trading yawns the way people do, which makes me laugh.

When there is sufficient light I look at her carefully, to see that she has no wounds or injuries. I gauge the strength of her bad leg. If we are lucky, other deer are nowhere to be seen, the world feels private and still and she is relaxed. This is crucial, as she is always on the alert. Having been the outcast and pariah, she has developed her flight instinct, listening for distant sounds, alert to scents. If another deer comes within a few hundred feet, Penelope can instantly become tense, nervous, frightened, depending on which deer it is, and if it is an enemy, she will begin to gulp her apples quickly, prepared to bolt. I try to calm her and tell her that I am with her and that she is safe.

I talk to her to strengthen our connection, and my voice appears to have a soothing effect. At a minimum, tone and feeling are present, as when we hear a foreign language, and while she obviously doesn't understand the meaning of most words, she does know the meaning of some. She gives a tail wag at the word "apples," another at the word "chestnuts." She knows "come." When she has food in her mouth and is asking for more, she understands the meaning of "chew what you've got." She will stop asking and fully chew and swallow her mouthful. I then ask "Is that down? All the way?" and when it is, she signals it by wagging her tail. She knows the phrase "take a break" and will back off from the feeding. She knows "let's sit down" and will carefully lower herself onto the grass next to my chair. It is comforting to read companionably while she is beside me and it perhaps gives her peace as well, for at such a moment she has been fed and is safe and protected. She also knows the meaning of "It's okay. I won't let anyone hurt you," visibly relaxing at the sounds. Her ability to respond to spoken communication feels all the more remarkable because of the innate silence amongst deer.

I place a variety of the best apples in her bowl—Honeycrisp, Kiku, Fuji, Envy. She is clear in her preferences, some kinds eliciting a passionate response, evident in her breathing and her eagerness to get

It may seem unlikely that a wild animal and a human could spring from similar, perhaps nearly identical root systems, and even less likely that they could then somehow find each other, but it happened.

as much as she can. I know her favorites, shop for her with enormous pleasure, and have chosen each piece of fruit to be as perfect as possible in form, size, and color. As I feed her, I speak the name of the type and start with one I know will please her. "Look what we have! An Ambrosia!"

With my pocketknife I cut a quadrant, then cut that slice into about fifteen bite-sized pieces. Holding the slices in my left hand, I take one piece in my right and extend it toward her mouth. She accepts it gently with her lips and tongue and in the same smooth motion, she takes my fingers into her mouth. She has learned to chew her food without biting me, and she likes to hold my fingers in her mouth until I give her the next piece. If all she wanted was the apple, she could simply take it, chew, swallow, and prepare for the next. The holding of my fingers is related to the food, yet it is distinct and seems as strongly desired, perhaps an echo of the nursing she needed from her mother but was denied. She wants the contact, the touch, the feel of my hand. Piece by piece I feed her the whole apple. Then she licks both of my hands, backs and palms, licks all my fingers, my wrists, and forearms, and the grooming seems to provide her extended comfort.

I select another, a different variety, and feed it to her in the same way. When she has eaten all its pieces, including the core, the seeds, and the stem, I select another. It is reasonable to assume that her sense of taste is as keen as her sense of smell, the two being linked. Penelope lets me know that, as good as the others are, the flavor of New Zealand Kikus, available for only a few weeks each year, is superior. She gets a wild look in her eyes at the taste of them. She will go for my left hand to try to take all the pieces at once. I tease her slightly, giving her one bite at a time, telling her to not eat too fast, that it's all for her, she will get the whole thing, no one will steal from her.

I have observed reflexive cruelty toward Penelope on the part of certain deer who chase her, especially two adult females, one the mother of the twins, whom I have named Castle for her crenelated white foot markings. Penelope flees from them, a grossly uneven match. She can move semi-quickly when she is frightened, at the cost of significant pain, running on a broken foot. The pursuing deer, being stronger, larger, and healthier, will trot or canter after her, not letting up until Penelope has been chased quite a distance. They do not seem to want to catch her or harm her physically, the chase is a signal of dominance, a message that she is not wanted, yet the threat of injury must be enough that Penelope is terrified. I have sometimes seen her approach the property, and as she nears, one of the aggressors bound out at her. Penelope turns and runs, her pivot at too great a distance for me to intervene. I have tried to teach her that if she comes toward me, she will be safe, but that if she heads away I will be unable to help and she will be vulnerable. It is her instinct to flee. Yet when she gets chased away, in a few minutes she returns via a different pathway. She does not give up, and her subsequent attempts must require courage, knowing that an enemy is potentially preventing her access to me.

On these reapproaches I meet her and escort her, greet her with extra warmth and tell her I'm sorry for what happened. I have shown her several times that I will protect her, charging toward a deer that is threatening her, shouting at it until it runs. Penelope has gradually gained assurance that if she stays close to me, I will not allow harm to come to her. When she feels safe, she relaxes and we enjoy our private time. When she is ready to leave, she moves gradually to the edges of the property, stopping to look back. Seeing that I am watching her, she will pause, then move a bit farther away. Although she approaches directly, she leaves indirectly, in stages. Once she is out of sight, I am free to go in, get another cup of coffee, and start my workday. If the day involves meetings or anything else which takes me away from the house, I try to schedule it so that I will be home and ready for her evening return.

As with our mornings, at the end of the day I scan the woods for her. When we see each other toward evening I can often tell that she is agitated, worn out, tense, fearful. I have no way to know what has happened in the ten or twelve hours we have been apart. In the woods she may have been bullied by other deer. Perhaps angry homeowners have yelled at her and chased her for eating their flowers. Maybe she has been barked at by dogs, had close calls with cars, been blasted by horns. Whatever the source of her stress, the level of adrenaline she has produced feels measurable. Almost certainly her broken leg has been giving her pain, and I can gauge her degree of discomfort in the way she moves, in her breathing and in her eyes. Some days it is clearly severe. If she has had a hard day she may be in no mood for subtleties. She is hungry and wants her dinner. It is much as it is with people—at such times she is more tolerant of my touch than desirous. But to give her anything at all is my pleasure, and when she is done eating she goes off to whatever place she chooses, to spend her night in peace.

The nature of love

Summer progressed, and day by day Penelope's ease with me appeared to deepen. As we crossed the borders which had separated us, something in me broke open. I felt a love that was nearly unbearable, an inexpressible joy. She was giving me her trust. I was honoring her gift.

She had come to me, as the result of random movement, or propelled along an invisible path, and I had recognized her and reached out. In our distinct ways we had spoken to each other and had each evidently been understood. Had she continued as she was before we connected in the springtime, starved and sunken, parched, misshapen, and wounded, she might have been able to survive for a while longer, but it seems doubtful. I had sensed that she was near death. As she became healthier, I felt her gain a sense of her place and her worth, knowing that, as I promised, I was watching over her. I believe that, as much as the fact that I always had fruit waiting for her, it was the talking, the eye contact, an exchange of feeling as I told her that she was good and that she was beautiful that drew her back to me each day, approaching, yet at the same time holding herself in reserve, alert to any sign of betrayal. She was akin to a person who has been abandoned and abused, mistreated by those who might have loved her but did not.

I understood the fragility of Penelope's trust, and her desire for it. Trust had been precarious in my early life as well, and knowing its uncertainty and its many betrayals committed me to honor the gift that was growing between us. I was continually mindful that Penelope's mother had rejected her when she was a few weeks old and still nursing, when she was suffering the pain of a broken limb, and that she had been left alone to die. Trust may be the largest component of love. It would be hard to argue that any form of love can exist without it, and a state termed "love" between two souls, in the absence of mutual trust, must be founded on a degree of pathology.

It may be that once betrayed we never fully, or even partially, recover what has been lost. Betrayal of trust can inflict a profound wound. Sometimes we turn our backs, walk away, and never return.

As children we live in a circumscribed world with a small number of players and few choices. We may have no one to tell us that the game of betrayal is not the only thing there is, nothing to show us that there are places where, and people with whom, trust is honored, freely given, and reliable. And yet the importance of trust does not necessarily diminish or recede because we learn to live without it. Its absence may make the attainment more imperative and I have learned that it is better to live with nothing, and with no one, than to live in a trust-vacant situation. Any relationship, whether between partners, friends, family members, and more broadly between people and animals, will toxify in every aspect of connection, immediately or ultimately, when it is not founded on mutual trust.

It might be excusable to claim an inability to behave in a trustworthy manner, to offer the inability as bedrock, if one has come into the world in its absence, but such an exemption offers no gain. We can learn our greatest focus and our greatest strength from areas of deprivation.

Domestic animals have been selectively bred to maximize the inherent qualities which humans value, and it is commonplace to recognize a bond of trust between a domesticated animal and a person who cares for it. The pleasure some take in habitually pretending to throw a ball for a dog, laughing as the dog earnestly takes off in pursuit of a ball which has been withheld, is a self-annihilating pleasure. In time the dog will learn to expect betrayal and will no longer operate from the basis of trust which is one of the strengths of their species. The trust, which was the master's for the taking, will have been lost.

Trust between a human and an animal living in the wild is a categorically different thing. As Penelope and I navigated the tides of trust, she indicated by her actions that she knew I had a life and had feelings, as she did, that I was more than a dispenser of food. Penelope's self-awareness extended to an awareness of my parallel individuality. Her actions indicated that she recognized me as distinct from other humans, of whom she was wary. She knew I was an individual, capable of a range of actions, not all of which might be consistent. She knew on some level that my behavior toward her had motive, even if it was selfless. She also showed through her actions and reactions that our connection had evolved and contained the capacity to further evolve, that my own actions toward her had changed and could continue to change. Each day was not the same as the day before. A gain in trust, for example, was not a singular, closed event, but one which carried forward to the next day and to those days which would follow. Our experience of the other was cumulative and we both understood that for a gain in trust to become structural, its value needed to be jointly honored. And for each of us, the day had come when we knew an issue was under consideration, a moment had arrived for moving to the next level. I had never failed to feed her when she came to me. Every time I had offered apples, I had given her apples. She had never come to me and been ignored. I had never been too busy, had never promised her food and then given it to one of the others. I had never drawn her close and then done something to startle her or chase her away, never tried to touch her without permission.

  I had wanted her to trust me enough to take food from my fingers, had felt that there would be pleasures shared. I had offered the contact gently, periodically, without insistence. I hadn't and wouldn't try to force her, out of her hunger or need, to do anything she did not want to do. She could have gone on refusing and there would have been no consequence. I would not have stopped feeding her, would never have refused to place her apple slices on the ground. Each time she declined to take a piece from my fingers I immediately placed it where she preferred. Everything she had allowed herself to expect of me she had received, and it was likely that she had internalized that.

  I was witnessing the signs and signals conveyed by a wild animal to express the idea of a relationship with a human having its own forward motion. Had I not seen them, I would not have been able to imagine them, yet she showed me that in her eyes our connection had grown and advanced. In the deeper and less tangible realm of feelings, did she sense my joy upon seeing her become healthy? What could she tell from the sounds of my voice? Each day I would talk to

Penelope while feeding her, the conversation gently flowing while I named a few of the growing number of people who regularly asked after her. I would quietly speak to her about some of the people in my life who had shown an interest. "I told Meg, in Savannah, all about you today. I sent her your picture and she said you are very beautiful. I sent your picture to Kathie, who believes in you and every day thinks good thoughts for your health. Ruth McArthur, who lives all the way in San Francisco, wanted to know how you are. And I spoke about you with Dr. Schenkel. She knows everything about animals and maybe someday we will go to her. Imagine it. We could drive in the car, you could put your head out the window if you wanted, and we'd pull up at the vet. We'd go into the waiting room. The receptionist would say, 'Penelope is here for her check-up.'"

My voice always holds her attention, and she will never walk away while I am speaking. I talk to Penelope in a way which is ours alone and do not use the tone and vocabulary I would with another person, do not speak to her as I would speak to a dog. Accepting the degree of abstraction, conveyed by tone, I'll tell her if I've seen a documentary about animal life—"There's a guy out west who lives with a herd of wild turkeys"—that I'd seen a clip of a baby elephant frolicking in surf, any sort of content, allowing the sounds to sustain the connection. I would tell her what I'd learned about white-tailed deer. "I was reading today that whitetails, just like you, have been on Earth for nine million years. It is an incredibly long time. People like me have been around for a tiny fraction of that, nothing really, compared to you." All of this was text. The subtext and metatext were simpler: Penelope was no longer alone. She had a bond with another living being.

We studied each other. Because it was Penelope's survival at issue and at stake, it was to her benefit to learn to read and interpret my actions and feelings. She was good at doing those things. A few weeks into our relationship, I saw that if I tossed a piece of apple toward her and, through my miscalculation, the piece hit her muzzle, she understood that the slight discomfort had not been inflicted

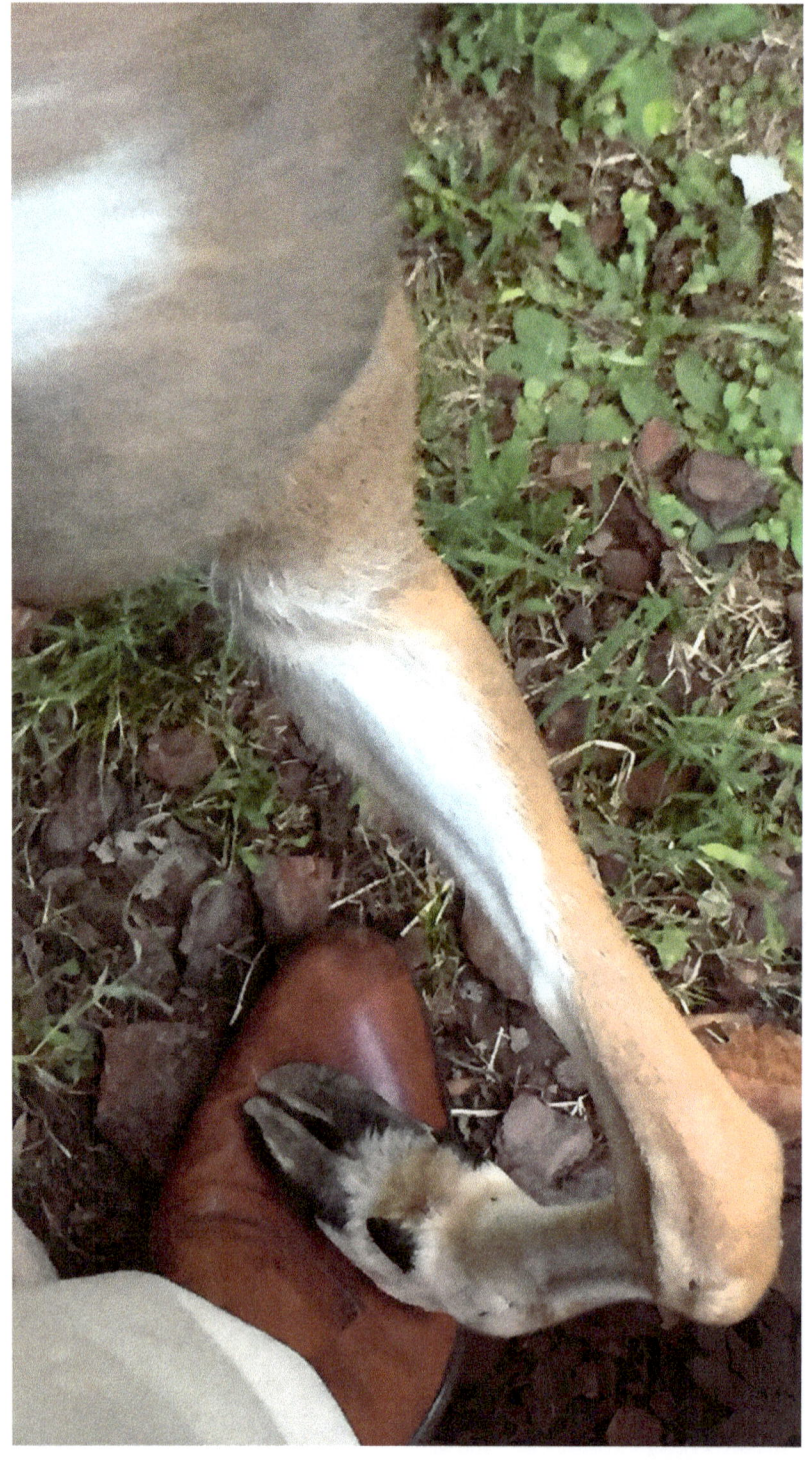

> *Trust may be the largest component of love. It would be hard to argue that any form of love can exist without it.*

deliberately. I had thrown it to her, not at her. She understood the distinction between intention and result. By the second week of August, if a piece of apple slipped from my fingers and landed in front of her, she would not pick it up but would stare at the apple and wait, knowing that the dropping was accidental. I would pick up the piece and she would eat it from my fingers. The eating-from-the-ground phase of our relationship was over. There seemed to be added satisfaction for Penelope in being fed by hand. Maybe she received the signals of my pleasure as I received them from her, another parallel to growing human intimacy. Whatever the components, much changed the week that Penelope began to eat from my fingers. We never regressed. She did not revert to being uneasy or mistrustful, and a sequential ritual was established. As soon as we were together, she went directly for my hand and held it in her mouth as long as she desired, usually several minutes. When we felt adequately reunited, I fed her. When the feeding was finished, then came her grooming of me. She would then stand in front of me and groom herself. When I sat in my chair, she would often sit on the ground beside me.

As I studied Penelope in repose, I wondered where inside her was the place that days earlier had still held some caution toward me, and which now held none. It must have been in her brain, but could the spot have been identified by MRI, comparing her earlier and current responses? The other parts of her which knew me differently included her tongue, the skin and hair of her muzzle, face, neck, head. The first time I reached and touched the top of her head she looked at me, as a person might, at a gesture of familiarity where explicit permission hadn't been given. There immediately came a second expression which said that she was just startled, it actually felt nice, and I could do it again if I'd like. Once we had done something for the first time, it was easy to do it again and it became part of our interaction.

Each morning I was up and outside in the dark, ready when she appeared, and I scheduled my day so that I'd be home for Penelope's evening visit. I refused every invitation that would have taken me away at the dinner hour. When, in late August, I learned that I would need to travel again to the West Coast, I wondered how long I could delay the trip, how briefly I might be able to stay away so I wouldn't interrupt the rhythm and the progress we were establishing. Apart from any sort of injury or accident afflicting her, the worst thing that could happen now was for the bond of trust to be violated. For Penelope to come to the house and find me gone, or, for all she knew, there but unresponsive, for her to feel that she had accepted me and that I had turned my back on her, that I had coaxed her to a point of connection and then disconnected, was something I would do a great deal to prevent.

In the boundaries which were being crossed, I sensed something being tested and proven, an area of belief becoming illuminated. Since childhood I had felt that, in life generally, those things which connect and unite us are greater and more substantial than those which separate and divide. My broad and reflexive belief that the lines of demarcation can be dissolved, and indeed that every form of goodness might flow from the dissolution, was now being demonstrated in the physical world. For so many years I had been thinking, and saying aloud, "Just break them down, sweep them away," in relation to divisions between individual men and women, to divisions of race, to religion—even as I would happily never again hear the word—in relation to every form of self-labeling and the labeling of others. To enable and witness such dissolution of boundaries has been my deep and strong hope. Here, it was happening on a tangible level. From Penelope's actions, from her body language and facial expressions, it appeared that we were feeling a similar bond. She touched me freely, playfully, evidently joyfully, at the same time I stroked her fur. It seemed we had both recognized that our commonality mattered more than our difference.

    Humans celebrate the existence of love, most of us experience it, yet it is a vexation causing as much pain as joy. We ponder love, struggle to find adequate words or images to describe it, turn over its subtleties and vagaries. We might be hard pressed to say what love is in any concrete sense, and may vaguely describe its origin, pointing to our hearts. It is easy to acknowledge that humans may fall in love with reflections of themselves, rarer and perhaps more meaningful to recognize kinship across lines not only of form but of substance, to feel a bond of oneness with a life of another species. And so the barrier between self and other can be mitigated. This is the ancient idea of the Peaceable Kingdom, the lion lying down with the lamb, a time-honored subject for painters and poets. We now delight in photos and videos of creatures of different species bonding with each other, of the predator protecting its historic prey, playing gently together, nestling, grooming, engaging in friendly or loving behavior.

    It becomes a stronger challenge to know that, while a pig might nurture a goat, a deer would reject her own fawn because of a deformity or incapacity. The two arenas of behavior seem at odds, yet it may be a more finely focused matter: the unavoidability of individuation. There may be loving and less loving souls everywhere in the animal world. We describe certain persons as being loving, describe their capacity to give love by degrees of magnitude and intensity—very loving, extremely loving—so it must be that by equivalent degrees, others are less loving, some not at all. There are individuals who are cold, distant, or cruel, not in an aberrant moment but as a continuous expression of temperament.

It is hard for me to comprehend Penelope's banishment by her mother. It is easy to recognize the love which took hold and grew between us.

Crossing the threshold

Seeing deer asleep in the snow, on a night where the temperature falls below zero Fahrenheit, I worry about them and admire their strength, knowing that in their place, without clothing, perhaps even with it, I would perish. Humans are not well equipped for survival. With our delicate feet and thin skin, lacking fur, quills, claws, scales, venom, or any other form of defense, much of what we produce is in recognition of our frailty. We are outliers, yet many of us have been persuaded of our exclusive value, taught to draw a categorical distinction between humans and all other creatures.

Some people, through empathy or philosophy, draw almost no distinction. Recognizing that taking the life of another human is the deepest sin, the greatest crime, they are unable to kill any animal directly or to be responsible for indirect killing, refusing to eat any form of meat or fish, to consume eggs or milk, to wear leather or fur, unable to trap a mouse or knowingly crush an insect. They develop and examine codes of conduct which feel intrinsic to them and are at ease with their place among the range of creatures.

Most of us, in our relation to other species, occupy an uncertain middle ground which can be littered with ambiguities and contradictions. We may become inarticulate if asked to explain how we can take the life of a spider but not of a kitten, eat a turkey but not a dog. Many who can yank a fish from the water and watch it die while it gasps in the air might be horrified by the sight of a horse being hooked through the mouth, hauled from the air, and held underwater until it drowned, although the two modes of death are precisely equivalent.

Through euphemism and abstraction, we are relieved of having to think about our inconsistencies and we adopt distancing tools to excuse ourselves from the examination of our values, referring to bacon or veal rather than pig or young calf, making it easier than it would have been in past centuries to evade the issues. A complex edifice has been constructed between the living creature and the rendered, reconfigured, and renamed food that lands on our plates. It is also easier today to live without killing or causing pain, and many people can rightly claim a compassionate and blameless life where other animals are concerned. Yet most of us take a middle path where we navigate our own systems of classification. We can see where, if not why, we draw our lines.

Harder to ascertain is how other life forms may perceive similarities and differences between themselves and us. Do wild animals identify us as the creatures that have cut down and paved over so much of their habitat, dirtied their water and air, the ones who make so much noise? They can't fail to recognize us as the ones who speed along in heavy, hard objects that maim and kill them in countless numbers. We cause harm and massive death, yet we are drawn to animals, to their appearance and behavior and there are reasons why so many humans choose to share our homes with them and why some feel a need to do so. To live beside a dog or cat, a bird or a horse, connects us to a spectrum of life.

I have shared parts of my life with several dogs, and the relative brevity of their time on Earth can be challenging. Seven weeks before Penelope was born, I buried Una, a mixed breed of such unfathomable intelligence and sensitivity that I could teach her almost anything by saying it once in a conversational tone and be permanently understood. Everyone

I knew treated Una with respect, there is no other word. She lived to be eighteen. They were good years, yet it is never enough, and her death followed too many others, from a variety of causes, some gentle, others not. At ten, I saw my childhood dog hit and killed in front of me on the Pacific Coast Highway. Hers was the first love of any kind I experienced, my first look at death, my first grief, and even now I cannot pass the spot where it occurred without fully reliving the moment, still blaming myself.

I presently have a loving Havanese named Monkey who has been growing blind and stays largely indoors where she can navigate. Through Monkey's increasing blindness I still take her for her afternoon walks along the shore of the Hudson. Within our walk, there is a quarter mile path where it is safe and I close my own eyes and walk blindly with her, to feel what she is feeling. I look forward to our shared blind walks, enjoying the empathy, and while I can't say how, I sense that Monk knows what is happening, trotting along in stride without even the slightest pulling or stopping as she does when my eyes are open.

And while it is uncommon, it felt natural that, years ago, I was given a newborn lamb to raise. The lamb had, in utero, been part of a pediatric medical experiment at a New York City hospital. A doctor friend, making sure she first received her mother's colostrum, smuggled her out of the hospital in a small cardboard box—the law mandated that ewe and lamb be killed upon birth—and she was in my hands at one hour old. I named her Stella, pure white, pink nose, and she took me as her mother, demanding her bottle every two hours—midnight, two o'clock, four— which I gladly warmed for her. The third-floor apartment was at first all she knew of the world, and she did remarkably well, running between the many connecting rooms at top speed, but when she grew to need a proper home with her own kind, I found one for her among a flock of thirty-five sheep. Every spring I would visit and at the sound of my voice she would run to me, all through her long life, the bond not forgotten.

Whether they come to us or are taken by us, domesticated animals largely live by our standards and by our rules. We cater to their needs, but they compromise their wild natures by accepting the bond in exchange for advantages of food, protection, and care. Perhaps selfishly, we look into the eyes of a cat or a dog, sense their acceptance, their tolerance or appreciation, and we feel enlarged. We feel strongly and feel much about them and take pride in ascertaining what they feel about us. Many of us class the love of an animal among the most precious experiences of our lives.

Acceptance and compromise sound reasonable, but tied, caged, or locked inside buildings, most domesticated animals have few choices. Many seem happy in their domesticity. When some manage to run away, notices are posted advertising a lost pet. Perhaps the pet does not want to be found, to be restricted again. It may have run from us in search of its true life.

Each living soul yearns to live in its own and rightful way, and to find that way, for ourselves and more particularly for each other, is a critical and noble task. While it may be difficult to recognize what the ways are, trying to understand them is possibly the truest expression of love. And just as every life must find its direction, just as there is no single pathway, so can there be discrepancies in how we perceive and feel about the forces at work in each of our worlds.

There is an argument that it is nature's way for a doe to reject her disabled fawn, an instinctual imperative of survival, not to be infused with human feelings. There follows a comparable assertion that humans are an evolved species in which such things happen differently, happen rarely, perhaps not at all. We often talk of maternal instinct as if it is as immutable as the motion of the tides, yet it is sometimes only moderate, sometimes minimal or absent, and there can be separation between a human mother and her child, the assumed bond negated.

My own instincts of nurturance and protection would not allow me to turn away from an instance of human maternal abandonment. And whether it is nature's way or not, I could not accept it in the life of an unwanted fawn.

The aspect of our physical contact that appears to be unique, separate from the deer's shared physicality, is Penelope's taking my fingers into her mouth and holding them there each time we approach one another.

Abandonment

It is notable that from the beginning Penelope showed no fear of me, that from the first time I approached, she let me come within a foot of her. To me, it felt as if we had already known one another, as if the relationship was in place, had already happened, and I accepted her presence as an inevitability. Her own willingness to allow me near may have been driven by her loneliness, having lived from her earliest days without her mother and siblings, without a herd. Prior to our connection, every time I saw The Girl with the Broken Foot, she was alone. When she approached me, I did not chase her away, I came toward her, fed her, looked upon her with kindness. Although I was not a deer, I was another living soul.

For months after I began to care for the disabled fawn, the only scenario I held was that of the mother abandoning the baby. Other possibilities could have presented themselves; the mother herself being injured or killed in the accident or the attack that injured her fawn. Perhaps a car had hit them both, running over the mother while only striking the leg of her fawn. The fawn then would have hobbled off the road and into the woods. It might have happened that way, but I think it is somehow the less plausible scenario, one which might ease my associated pain and let me off the uncomfortable hook. My research into whitetail deer confirmed that a disabled fawn would be abandoned by its mother. It seems the strongest likelihood, a supposition strengthened by something more easily observed and confirmed.

Without a mother, essentially unable to walk, the fawn was ostracized by the other deer in the area. At that time there was a herd of about a dozen adults and fawns. I came to learn just how small a range deer will choose to inhabit, a fact that would facilitate my connection to the fawn. As a mother will abandon an imperfect offspring, a herd will cull the unhealthy, weak, or lame through rejection, and I was able to observe that the mature females aggressively chased away the disabled fawn on sight. I again try to imagine the fawn, instinctively in need of the company of other deer, seeing them foraging together. She would approach, wanting to join, and would be driven off. In writing fiction, names of characters materialize unbidden and I have learned to accept the first name that appears, without a thought, to not second-guess. Time will often reveal that there was an unconscious reason for the name having arisen, with overtones and substrates, which show the instinctive name to have been right. I named Penelope intuitively. When eventually I did look it up, I was reminded that the name belonged to the wife of Odysseus, that she was the loyal partner who awaited her husband's return. What I never consciously knew was that the Penelope of Greek legend had been abandoned as an infant, left to die.

Penelope knows her name and comes when I call it. I wonder what form of identifier she has for me, an image of my face and body, the sound of my voice or the sound of her own name as I speak it, the smell of apples or the scent of my skin. I wonder what she makes of my clothing, which is similar from day to day, but not exactly the same. Aware of the limited range of a deer's color vision, their red-blindness and receptivity to cool colors, I try to choose tones and textures which approximate her own and avoid any pattern which might appear unnatural. There is one sweater she likes, of undyed pale grey-brown Shetland wool. She has often rested her face against my chest when I am wearing it and has repeatedly nibbled on the cuff of the right sleeve, appearing to take comfort, reminding me that she was denied the oral contact of grooming by her mother and siblings, and as often as possible, I wear this sweater when I know I will be with her.

While resting her head against my chest, Penelope has frequently stood with her front feet on mine. I try always to wear shoes which are familiar, one pair in particular—simple, earth-toned, unornamented—which have been present during most of our time together. One day I wore similar shoes which she had never seen. She stood at a distance, staring at them, and would not come any closer. I changed, she came, and I have never again worn them in her presence. By offering reliable sameness, I strive to allow her to feel comfortable and safe. Her fear and mistrust of the other humans is palpable, her trust in me has grown to be substantial and I do what I can to strengthen it.

On our own

As my commitment to Penelope's well-being grew, I might have wondered what in myself was being touched by her maternal abandonment and enforced solitude. I had long accepted my own abandonment anxiety, had indeed joked that the words I wanted on my gravestone were "Please Don't Go." I was in my thirties before I learned that, immediately after being born, I had been left with a stranger. I was the first of three, my birth an experimental experience, and while the arrival of offspring in mammalian life is usually an event, my mother's thinking may have been "I'll get to him later."

Growing up in Toronto, I accepted the degrees of self-sufficiency which were expected of me. I was sent to an elementary school on the far side of the city. At the ages of six and seven, to get home I would leave school alone, walk to the subway station, descend, wait on the platform for the train, take it to the correct station, go up to street level, get a transfer, board a bus, take it for miles, get off and walk the rest of the way uphill to the house. Toronto had real winters, was the largest city in Canada, and despite the often comical reputation of Canadians for being nice, probably not a completely safe place for a six-year-old child to wander. Today such parental casualness would be seen as odd but in earlier decades it was apparently less so. The very few times I found myself in a fix, I solved it myself and would never have thought to ask anyone for help.

At the age of eight I was told that we would be moving to Los Angeles, where my father, an actor, had been given a leading role in a network series. I must have seen this as an opening to begin my own adult working life. I wrote a letter to Walter Alston, manager of the L.A. Dodgers, applying for a job as a bat boy. I perhaps had misunderstood the word "boy" as I did not receive the expected enthusiastic reply. I had imagined that I would go on the road, traveling with the team, that I would have been exempted from attending school, that my parents would have been relieved of any responsibility, given that I would have had my own income, and that, checking in periodically, I would be free to live my own life.

Some part of me already knew that work would be self-protective. By the time I was twelve, I was making money as a musician in L.A. and while a student in junior high school, largely taking care of myself.

Getting up alone every morning at six, I showered, dressed, made breakfast, and left the house without seeing another soul. I have never since allowed anyone to start their day alone, without my attention and companionship, and I am always awake and ready to care for Penelope on her schedule. While we share specific means of communication, even if I wanted to I cannot give her to understand that on any morning I might have had a sleepless night, am tired and cannot get up to provide her expected breakfast. I cannot tell her I am sorry, we are out of fruit, but that I will get her some later in the day. To sustain the relationship, I must fulfill her needs. I am there for her, as and when she expects me to be, and the wonder resides in that by doing so, my own needs are fulfilled.

In giving to Penelope without reciprocal demand, by overriding what had befallen her, by unraveling her rejection and wanting her never to be alone, every piece feels to be in its proper place.

Standing up for her

Early one morning in May, as I was waiting for her, Penelope came hobbling across the lawn as fast as she could. Right behind her, chasing her, was Castle. Penelope drew close and stood beside me, breathing hard. I got up, held out both hands toward her in a gesture of reassurance, and said "It's okay. You stay here. I'll take care of this."

I turned and placed myself between Penelope and Castle. Facing the larger doe, inches from her, I pointed a stern finger at her and, wanting my tone to convey intention, said firmly "You can't be mean to her. You cannot chase her. You have to be nice."

Looking at me unresponsively, Castle did not flinch. I repeated the warning. Nothing. From observing the deer, I had learned some of their physical vocabulary, particularly one dominance gesture which, between themselves, appears always to be effective. Standing squarely in front of Castle, I slowly raised my right leg and swiftly brought my foot straight down hard, stamping the ground. She looked at me, her eyes widened, she instantly turned, bolted, and kept running.

The action requires two strong front feet: one to stamp, the other to support the body, a gesture Penelope may have yearned to use but is incapable of. During this, she had been standing a few inches behind me, like a child whose parent is confronting the neighborhood bully. I turned toward her. I had stood up for her, and I had done it in the deer's own language.

She had seen that in addition to providing food, I am her protector. Our knowledge of the other had deepened. Some part of the separation between our species had been breached. Driving away a threatening deer with cervine body language had felt miraculous to me. I can only surmise how it might have felt to Penelope. She had an expression I had not seen before. We moved a few steps to the small table, where I fed her. She stayed with me a long time.

The next morning as Penelope and I were outside, Castle came around, walking along the property line. She saw us together and gave us a wide berth.

In ways that none of the other deer have, she has struggled with physical pain, and with rejection, aggression and solitude.

Clarity

What draws us toward another life? It may be a desire for completion. It may be a form of self-recognition. We remark that couples often resemble one another, yet it is striking how direct the resemblances can be. To browse the Times on Sunday and see photos of those betrothed can be humorous, with some couples who appear to be siblings or even fraternal twins. Sometimes they share a highly singular feature—an unusually shaped mouth or nose, a tilt of brow—that distinguishes each of them from most other people but may have been exactly the thing that drew them to the other.

And this forces me toward a troubling thought.

The longer I observe the deer in the area, the more I see variations of feature, proportion, and coloring within the species. Each family of whitetails, up and down the road, has its own distinctive familial look and set of characteristics in their bodily configurations and coloration. A small herd who live half a mile away all have dark faces, light circles around their eyes, and black center stripes on their outer tail surface. They look much like each other, and different from the deer who live in this immediate area.

Penelope looks very much like the two I call the twins, born at the same time she was. Photos of Penelope and Daisy side by side reveal great similarity. Daisy's late brother, Anthony, resembled not only Daisy, he also very closely resembled Penelope.

I may have been mistaken to assume that the three fawns appearing in the deer sanctuary at the same time were born to two mothers. In truth, I never saw the doe I assumed to have been Penelope's abandoning mother. I may have been entirely wrong in thinking that her mother walked away from her. Where would she have gone? Whitetails tend to live in the same small area all their lives. A doe with an injured fawn would be less likely to take herself away than to drive away an unwanted burden.

It seems increasingly possible that there were not two does giving birth to a set of twins and a single fawn. Penelope may have been one of triplets born to Castle. Over the past year, Castle has been the most cruel to Penelope, violently and viciously chasing her away. If Castle were merely the mother of the twins, why would she harbor such strong rejection of an unrelated, disabled fawn who was attempting to browse and to rest in the same small area as her two accepted offspring? If Penelope were not her fawn, why would Castle have such passionate antipathy?

Having looked at the available evidence, I must now accept that Penelope is Castle's daughter. Before I knew I was doing so, I had placed myself in the literal center of the drama of a mother rejecting her child. The impulse behind the mother's rejection was not negligence or apathy. The rejection was fueled by brutality. While Castle has watched us, I have nurtured Penelope, fed her by hand, stroked her, and received her own gestures of affection. I have not only been caring for her, I have been protecting an innocent life from a cruelly predatory and rejecting parent.

Castle is capable of seriously wounding me—an adult deer's hooves are sharp, their legs immensely strong, able to rip and trample a person to death—yet to protect Penelope I have run toward Castle, yelling in her face, placed myself in her path as she charged toward her own offspring. Her energetic rage was stunningly palpable. Armed with nothing but my voice and my commitment to Penelope's protection, I drove Castle away. In the triad of deer, fawn, and human, I had effectively taken the role of Penelope's mother.

When multifaceted evidence was right before me, I had been blind to the truth that Penelope is Castle's fawn, but once I had the key it was obvious: There had been a triple birth. At some early moment, Penelope had become injured and was driven away from her family. Two fawns were accepted, and one was rejected. Later, when chased by her mother, Penelope would struggle down the embankment, across the road and into the woods, where she would remain to survive alone. I could not understand that I was witnessing periodic repetitions of Penelope's initial banishment. The remaining two triplets, Daisy and Anthony, were allowed to claim this property as their base through the summer and fall of 2014 and the following winter. Unknowingly, I supported the situation. It is painful to acknowledge that Penelope, if she had been observing from a distance, may have witnessed me feeding her mother and siblings while she herself had nothing, and no one, through the barren months of that forbidding winter.

I wish I found it incomprehensible that any mother could treat a child with concentrated aggression and focused rage, yet the dynamic is familiar to me, which may explain why I was blinded to it in Penelope's case. The night in March when Penelope appeared outside, she was returning to the place of her birth and the place where her family resided without her, perhaps in the hope that she would be taken back by her mother. Castle was not here that night, but I was. I welcomed Penelope home.

Opening to her

My relationship with Penelope could only have happened because I had learned to relinquish myself in an instinctual way, allowing uncommon levels of connection with other people. By simply being in the world and being still, people have approached me, in search of reflection, compassion, a safe place to confess or to cry, wanting to talk. A phrase I have heard many times, from strangers, is "I've never told this to anyone." In this way, bonds have been formed, some of which developed and sustained over years. I don't know what Penelope may have sensed when she came to me. I was open to her presence as I had learned to be open to others. It was unique only in that she was a wild animal. In every other way it was part of a continuum and it seemed a matter of detail rather than of essence that she and I were of different species. Internally, I took away the things that separated us, my attention directed at her place in the moment and what she needed of me.

Our alliance was not something I could have willed to happen, could not have forced it to happen or even encouraged it. I could only have accepted it as it was given. In opening myself to Penelope I was able to shed not only my identity as an individual but to some extent my identity as a human. Seeing her, a few months old, making her way alone through her first forbidding winter may have set up sympathetic vibration, chiming echoes of being alone as a young child. And while I did not know what had happened to break her leg, I did know what had happened to break each of mine, in separate accidents years apart, the first at the age of nine, riding a horse that fell and landed with its full weight on my left leg. I had then, for some time, been unable to walk properly, had known pain and impediment which, while perhaps less severe than hers, were unavoidably related.

The second accident, in young adulthood, was of great value and I would not undo it. I was hit by a car on my bicycle, scooped off the pavement on a stretcher, placed in an ambulance, wheeled into surgery for a four-hour operation to reconstruct my right hip and femur, and kept a month in the hospital. When finally released I spent months on crutches before being able to use both legs.

Once home, I immediately got back to work, standing all day on one leg to paint, happily walking five miles each afternoon on crutches, with only my left leg allowed to touch the ground. I felt the intensity of being alive more sharply than at any other time, aware that an inch one way or the other could have brought life to an end, feeling everything that followed as a gift, liberating me in ways I only partially understood but keenly felt.

In the aftermath of being struck I had been forced to relinquish my will, to submit, with no power to change anything. I could not have gotten up from the pavement, could not have refused surgery, opting to tough it out, could not have left the hospital no matter how I wanted to see the sky. Surrender was the only option, an open acceptance of what the moment had brought, a lesson that might not otherwise have arrived. I came to feel that time would almost always bring experience more valuable than I would have chosen, that its worth might be folded into the moment, invisible at first but ultimately revealed, eliciting gratitude. Having relinquished my will in one circumstance, I was able to do it broadly. In painting I felt the work coming through me rather than from me. I began feeling the same forces at work in life.

I awaken each morning wondering "what's going to happen today?" And things happen. By the evening Penelope arrived I was prepared to set aside my sense of self, to devote my attention to her and to the most rewarding question I know: "Who are you?"

Eugenics

While her mother wishes her gone, or wants her dead, I love Penelope. Genetics may play a part. In an evolutionary sense it may be logical that a doe, and by extension a herd, would try to rid itself of an imperfect specimen, survival of the fittest being one of nature's goals. In the same evolutionary sense, as taboo as it is to address, it may be understandable that a human parent can reject, neglect, and perhaps wish dead a child deemed imperfect, less fit for survival. Yet we pride ourselves on a capacity to rise above and circumvent aspects of our animal nature. While we can impulsively copulate with attractive strangers, we class it as an aberration, tell ourselves that by organization we are capable of refinement, that we carefully select mates, are faithful to them and resist primal, animalistic urges. But some parents reject and seek to rid themselves of their children, by indirect or direct means. When it happens, we seek to ascribe psychiatric or biochemical disorder as its root cause, asserting that any mother or father who so treats an innocent child must be off their meds, must be suffering from depression, schizophrenia, bipolar disorder, fill in the psychotic blank.

Yet seemingly healthy people can behave in related ways, finding means to disguise their treatment of their children, careful to stop short of identifiable damage and cruelty, the punishments less visible, sometimes diabolically subtle.

Many people walk through life with wounds of parental rejection and are primed to continually find extended rejection in the larger world. Of those, how many seek solace and love from dogs and cats? How many solitary souls appear to have no one to love them except a creature of a different species? Indeed, when we soften at a video of a goat nestling into the side of a horse, we may credit the better nature of the animal world. Maybe it is only a manifestation of the wounded needing to heal, finding the protective impulse in a different creature because that nurturing soul has no evolutionary stake in the survival of the damaged young one. Why would a horse reject a goat? For no reason. The goat's survival will not reflect upon the horse's place on earth or biological fitness, will not degrade the health of the herd or of equine kind in general.

Many of us describe the love between ourselves and domesticated animals as pure and simple, felt to a profound degree, celebrated joyfully over the course of shared years, mourned passionately when the loved one is lost. The love between a human and an animal is unfettered by much of what makes human love complicated, painful, perhaps unattainable. Inter-species love may be as powerful as it is in part because there is no evolutionary stake; familial and species narcissism are not in effect. We might view our domesticated animals as reflecting upon our worthiness, our status, our fitness, but only to a social and not to a biological degree.

Some years ago, walking into my parents' living room, I saw on the piano a small framed photograph which had been obscured, overlaid with another photographic print. The visible image was of my parents' dog. The photo it was hiding was of my brother, my sister, and myself. It was not one of several photos in the room depicting their children, it was the only one.

The abrasions and the more quietly conflicted emotions which simmer and surge between men and women, between parents and children, between siblings, between friends, may be an extension of biological aspiration, all of us feeling that we might have done better than we have done, that to do better is vital to our survival. The drifting apart, the eventual losses of affection and appreciation, the loss of love, may be the visible tip of an evolutionary drive which continually impels us to strive to exceed our limitations. Parents who harbor secret or overt disappointment in their children might feel that a child's academic, social, or economic status reflects upon their own. Our pets, no matter their looks or intelligence, can stimulate an uncorrupted capacity for love. If they are impaired or disabled, comical looking, seemingly daft, our devotion to their comfort and survival ennobles us. We proudly state "He's a rescue."

I may be to Penelope what a dog is to a wounded and lonely person; a creature offering protection and companionship, each of us rejoicing in the simple presence and well-being of another life.

*I stand in the cold
or the rain if she is
standing in cold or
rain, and I feel no
hunger, thirst, cold
or wetness. I feel
the satisfaction that
she is eating when
hungry, that she is
getting what she
enjoys the most.*

Things happen

SEPTEMBER 8

I went out at five thirty this morning to wait for Penelope, but the first to show up by herself was Daisy. She stood shyly in front of me, I fed her a couple of apples, and she wandered toward the front of the house. Penelope then arrived, we had our usual morning time, and when she went off, I went in. At eight o'clock I looked outside and saw Daisy, in the deer sanctuary, giving birth.

It took a moment to realize what I was seeing, and another to realize why it felt so odd. Fawns are born in the spring, from mid-May into early June. Today was the second week of September. I took photos of the fawn through the window. Going outside, I could hear the fawn bleating and, following the sound, I went to the driveway, where the baby was hobbling on its new legs, turning toward me, and back to the foliage where Daisy stood watching.

I now have someone new to worry about, a fawn born in the fall, well outside the natural order. I easily named the fawn September, good enough whether female or male. I don't know its chances for survival, with cold weather coming. He or she will still be small by the first frost, unable to grow a winter coat. Daisy has always been different and it is so like her to have this happen. Calculating the whitetails' average gestation of 201 days, delivering her fawn on September 8 means that she became pregnant around February 19, when she was only seven months old.

Back in mid-February, there had been a pair of bucks hanging around. I had seen them following Daisy, chasing her, during a period of several days, but I gave it little attention because of the season and because she was young. I was wrong. Nursing her fawn, Daisy will be out of contention for the rutting period due to begin in October. It leaves Penelope as the only available female in the immediate area. If one or more bucks set their sights on her they may view me as a rival, should they come upon us during our feeding time. A rutting buck is single-minded in the pursuit of females and it will necessitate caution on my part.

As for September, I quietly commit to do my best, to watch over this slender, lithe new body, which seems so fine, fragile, and flexible as to be almost weightless.

SEPTEMBER 11

Early this morning Daisy came and I fed her. I haven't seen her with her fawn since the birth Tuesday and can only hope that she is hiding September in a safe spot. Daisy has always seemed passive and perhaps somewhat dim, but instinct and intelligence are separate things. My anticipatory concern for the survival of this very late arrival does not let up, even as there is little I can do.

Penelope did not appear this morning, the first morning in a long time that I haven't seen her. A possible reason emerged when a trio of bucks wandered onto the property, all three staying together at a distance. They are the first adult males I have seen since last winter and I have no idea where they have been these many months or where they have emerged from today. The separation of the sexes is all but absolute, the adult males living and moving together, even as they are in competition.

If Penelope conceives and gives birth next spring it will be an expression of her survival, overcoming her punishing start. I visualize her approaching early one morning, followed by an unsteadily prancing fawn of her own. It would be a triumph; not just one life saved, but enlarged and extended to bring more life to the world. The bucks are the key to that and I should of course welcome them.

I have no way to know whether Penelope's disability will impact her desirability, but with Daisy nursing her own late fawn, in the immediate area Penelope is it. Life will unfold.

And life unfolds. I received my wish to hold September's fine and weightless body. Late this afternoon I found her by the side of the road, still warm, her eyes with the vacancy of death, as I have seen it too many times. I lifted her and carried her up the same driveway where she had taken her first steps. I buried her where I had first seen her, near where she had been born, where so many of the others, including her mother, had been born. It is a very small grave. I had watched over her all her life, which lasted three days.

Vulnerability

Penelope comes and goes at her will, not in concert with mine, and except in those hours when she is with me, I cannot protect her. Her ability to remain safe, to avoid danger, exists apart from my protective impulse. In the moment I set eyes on her, when she is coming to me, my pleasure is mixed with relief, highlighting my fear that she might have been hurt, perhaps hit by a car in the night. A coyote, or a pack of them, could have come upon her while she slept beside the lake, and while any deer would be vulnerable, she is particularly defenseless. When threatened she is able to run, but poorly.

Her left front hoof is entirely disabled, the right one partially so, and they are a doe's natural weapons. When she has run to me, chased by her mother, I have protected her, but until I can see her, touch her, care for her, I have no way to know where she is, and whether she is safe and free of pain. On the rare morning or evening that she fails to show herself I become suffused with worry. Having missed her last night and again this morning, my thoughts are that I will never see her again, that the bucks chased her, that she ran, perhaps to me and I wasn't here, or that she ran into the road. And I know that if I see her this evening, I will feel great relief, and that it will last only as long as she is with me. I should have faith in her natural instincts and relax in her occasional absences; she has always returned.

Each time we are together she nuzzles her head into my chest and abdomen, rubs her chin and the sides of her head against me, and then inserts her muzzle between my body and right arm, running it up and down. It has become a ritual which grows more effusive and has taken on a playful aspect. Penelope seems to feel it is as important a part of our time together as the feeding. And again, examining whether I am projecting my feelings and concepts of behavior onto a wild animal, I think about it from as many vantage points as I can. Rather than being compared to human standards, her behavior can be compared to and contrasted with itself. Over the months, our daily interaction has evolved linearly, the changes initiated by her. I have been careful in making the feeding reliable and not contingent upon her behavior. She has not had to perform to receive her apples. No matter how she has chosen to interact with me, no matter at which distance or in which manner, she has gotten fed. It could have continued indefinitely as it began, without any enhanced closeness or contact, but we now share a very different set of behaviors than we had even two months ago. The reliable and repetitive nature of the contact indicates that it is not random, accidental, or capricious. She initiates the touching.

Observing the ways deer interact with each other, I see clear signs of love between mothers and fawns. After a fawn has nursed, the mutual grooming begins. The first minutes of licking serve to keep the other clean, free of insects and extraneous plant matter. As the grooming continues, it takes on a different character, mother and fawn closing their eyes while they lick. Sibling fawns do the same with each other upon greeting and at other, seemingly random times, and I cannot interpret it as anything but affectionate.

Penelope included me in this grooming behavior when sufficient trust was established to not only accept food from my hand but to want it that way. Her expressions of trust and affection emerged together. Every test we apply to feelings to know their true nature—and it may seem humorous to engage in comparisons with human adolescence—to ask ourselves as we do when young whether our feelings might be merely infatuation or physical attraction, whether we would experience

that wrenching sensation of heart and soul for another person if one or more things were different, leads to a reductive state. It does the same here and there can be no other term applied to my joyful connection with Penelope—it is love.

    Love is an enduring theme in individual human affairs, yet it can be elusive and is perhaps rarer than we admit. The word "love" is used in a broad range of circumstances and, if used promiscuously, it loses value. But I think love can be defined as concern for the well-being of another. And if another's well-being is our primary concern, to the degree that our own individual well-being takes second place, the possibility of love between one life and another finds a foothold, a place to flourish. The self-sacrifice involved in healthy and productive loving mandates that the safety and health of another take precedence over our own. It may seem a given but is far from the norm.

    Penelope has long shown confidence that I would not hurt her in any physical way. Yet she waited, needing to be secure in her assurance that if she accepted me I would not reject or abandon her, that I would not behave as her mother had done. The trust she sought to establish was not physical. It was emotional.

SEPTEMBER 16

This evening at sunset, after a session of feeding followed by lengthy cuddling of her head into my chest and arms, I gave her the hand gesture for "let's rest." I sat in my chair. She lowered herself to the ground a few feet away. We rested in the fading light. She kept looking at me, from time to time raising her chin, a gesture I answered in kind. When she rose, I got up as well, cut another apple, and fed it to her.

Then she lifted her injured foot to me. An hour earlier I had touched it lightly with the backs of my fingers as I bent to pick up a fallen piece of apple. Although she had taken to resting the injured foot on the top of my right shoe, I had never before touched it with my hand. I wondered if she had noticed the touch. Now she was extending the twisted foreleg at the level of my hand, but before there was any contact, she had an abrupt reversal reaction, putting the leg down and coming toward me with something that felt like aggression. I was startled and backed away a step. She came toward me again. I told her "No lunging" in a tone she seems to understand. She then had what seemed to be a small seizure, scuttling backwards spasmodically, her entire body contorted. It lasted three or four seconds, paused, repeated, then ended as quickly as it had come.

She went about browsing. I was disturbed by her sudden shift of affect and seeming loss of control. In the first few days of our physical contact in August she had displayed a similar, conflicted gesture toward me which felt as if it might be either playfulness or aggression. Each time I had observed the uncontrolled, backwards twisting scuttle, it had followed what seemed to be an increased gesture of trust and intimacy on her part.

I looked up "epilepsy" and "seizures in whitetail deer" and could find nothing. Hours later I lay awake, troubled, wondering whether it was her fear reaction, or perhaps a surge of adrenaline brought on by emotion—her increased desire to trust me—and a compensating panicked withdrawal. She has taken a risk in allowing me complete contact. Her caution and apprehension in the months leading to our first touches were probably an expression of my otherness and, although overcome in a relatively brief time, might still reside within her. Her broken foot is, in every sense, a sensitive body part, a source of pain, and quite possibly a source of emotions comparable to those experienced by a disabled person.

SEPTEMBER 17

After last evening's strange episode, I was eager to see Penelope and wondered whether our contact would resume normally. For the first morning in a very long while, she did not come. Whatever transpired last night, whatever its nature and cause may have been, it felt to me that something had changed, and perhaps she felt the same.

Day by day we have each taken the measure of the other. Penelope has a range of behaviors and emotions and I am worried that she might at the moment not trust me, that we might have sustained damage. I am reminded of people who have negated or walked away from relationships precisely because they were afraid of loss, afraid the relationship would fail. Such forced endings often follow an increased level of intimacy, perhaps a sudden and unexpected deepening of feeling,

which brings with it the fear of vulnerability. To end something because we are afraid it will end, to instigate loss from fear of losing, may seem paradoxical but is not uncommon.

If Penelope were to walk away and never return, she has as a model the separation from her mother at a very tender age. She must or may carry memory of such a foundational event, cognitively, emotionally, unconsciously, metabolically. Offering her wounded foot to me, she may have been expressing a desire to have me touch her most vulnerable part, to heal the pain. I have been wanting to do exactly that, and the possibility that she might have thought I could hurt her is hard to bear.

I had gone the entire day yesterday without seeing Penelope. Last night I waited until dark, with no sign. But this morning, as it was getting light, she came.

It may be true that an animal that has been abandoned, malnourished, abused, or imperiled does not forget the experience. Some believe that a dog which has been rescued never loses its appreciation and gratitude toward the adoptive master. Maybe every bowl of food, every loving touch, each kind word, the feel of a soft bed at night, carries greater pleasure and meaning than it would have had there been no deprivation.

A person who has suffered abuse and deprivation may have seen too much of humanity's potential to ever accept a gesture of kindness or love without caution. For a complex of reasons, some prefer and embrace the abuse. An abused child may not know that the world offers

> *Day by day we have each taken the measure of the other.*

anything different. They may feel they deserve the unkindness, acceptable because it is reliable. Abuse is probably not love in disguise, whereas the appearance of kindness can easily mask cruelty. The victim of cruelty can be confident that further cruelty awaits them. Absence of trust is a similarly settled matter.

Penelope comes to me, knowing that I will be kind. She touches me freely and allows me to touch her. She extends her trust, not only repeating the experience of the previous day but enlarging its parameters. On the day she first ate from my fingers, she may have accepted that for four months I had never done anything to cause her harm or alarm, had stood between her and her aggressive mother, had protected her and shown my commitment to her safety and her well-being.

Penelope has seen that she is not one of several deer who eat from my hand, that she alone receives such care and attention from me. I believe that this exclusive position is important to her. And while my belief might be seen as an imposition of human feeling, there is evidence for it. She exhibits anxiety if I feed anyone else. She is clearly most at ease—I will use the word happiest—when she and I are alone together, perhaps one reason for her very early morning appearance, before the others are out and about.

When she is beside me, she is vigilant for the sound, scent and sight of other deer. If Daisy wanders over, Penelope starts to grab for the apples, nervous that I will give away some of her food. Indeed, I will toss bits to Daisy, for several reasons. I have cared for Daisy all her life and she is entitled to continuity of care. I also wish to encourage her companionship with Penelope, which I work to nurture, so that Penelope will have at least one friend. Daisy has also suffered losses, of her twin brother last winter, and of her three-day-old fawn, born so bizarrely out of season this month. Daisy is submissive and nonthreatening, and I feed her and Penelope together; Daisy at a distance, eating her apples from the ground. Penelope continues to eat from my hand when Daisy is present, but she is clearly unsettled and will occasionally chase Daisy, who defers to her and sprints a few yards away. When Penelope and I have an hour or two without any other deer or people in sight, she relaxes. She will stay with me after the feeding, the two of us slowly moseying around the yard.

This displays another kinship with a specific human emotion, one we often denigrate because jealousy and possessiveness are regarded as signs of weakness, or lack of emotional maturity. Jealousy may be a weakness, but it is not confined to humans.

SEPTEMBER 27

As mating season grows near, Penelope's visits are becoming irregular. She did not come at all this morning, but appeared this evening, as it was almost dark, slightly cautious in her approach and I think that her instincts are directing her away from me and toward the bucks. As she began to eat from my fingers, the ease and closeness were quickly reestablished. After a few minutes, as I bent to pick up a fallen piece of apple, I gently stroked her injured leg and she allowed several soft passes of the backs of my fingers over the twisted, broken joint.

SEPTEMBER 28

Last night's touching of her broken foot and lower leg released permission and a seeming desire for more. This morning, I fed her from a crouching position, as I sometimes do, rather than standing, putting us eye to eye, nose to nose. For the first time she touched my face with her own. It was a tentative, glancing touch, the same way she first touched my torso with her nose and lips a few weeks ago.

The October rut will soon begin and I am hoping that Penelope's disability won't be an impediment to her mating. It is hard to imagine her bearing the weight of an adult male upon her back, even briefly, without her leg collapsing, and maybe it will. Having a fawn of her own will be an affirmation of survival, a corrective to her solitude. She will nurse, clean, and care for it, and the fawn will bond with her, forming a pair for at least a year, after which Penelope might give birth to twins and her family life will be established.

I wonder whether her relationship with me may interfere with her receptiveness to a buck or alter her desirability to them, and if physical contact with me changes her smell. If she withdraws from me, partially or wholly, for whatever time is needed for the natural sequence to take its course, I will of course ease off, but would never initiate the separation, could not rebuff her, refuse her the daily feeding and contact, would never knowingly be seen as rejecting.

Our days are notably shorter, the nights cool. Penelope's tawny summer coat is almost completely shed, revealing her new grey coat, and she will again be shaggy. She seems healthy, has filled out, her walking is stronger, the damaged leg seeming almost sturdy at moments, even in its misshapenness. As my vet had predicted, she is learning to adapt. I like to think that her strengthening is not simply physical, that she has a sense of place in her own world, and that she feels she has a partner and companion in me. I believe that the other deer, having seen Penelope being touched, fed, and protected, have altered their attitudes and have accepted her, at least in my presence and perhaps away from it. Sometimes, as I feed her, I say "Your mother missed out on a good thing. She didn't know what she had, the best fawn in the world. She is the big loser. Just look at the good time we're having this morning."

SEPTEMBER 30

As I began to feed Penelope her breakfast, her mother and two younger fawns arrived. They stood a few yards away and watched as Penelope was fed by hand, as she licked me, and had her face, head, and neck stroked. I threw pieces of food to each of them and they had a taste of what Penelope was being given in abundance. She stood with me and we continued our feeding, her privileged position acknowledged by all.

The one who had been abandoned, rejected, outcast, scorned, and chased was today the princess, the beloved.

Paul Bochner

As new life begins

Moving straight toward me in a purposeful manner, Penelope appeared this morning, coming close and standing with me, almost touching. I saw a young male gently following her onto the property. Penelope's eyes had an unusual look. The buck stood a dozen feet away, watching as I fed her. I threw him pieces of apple from time to time, which he ate without taking his eyes from Penelope. When she was done eating, she sat down at my feet, as if she were showing the young buck that this property was her home, and that she had her own human. The male did not move from his post, the three of us at ease. After about twenty minutes, Penelope rose and she and I slowly walked over to the buck. It felt as if she were introducing me to her date. The two of them stood side by side for a few moments, then they went off together, toward the woods. In this simple and direct way, perhaps I have facilitated Penelope's first mating and I am hoping the buck will provide her the fawn I so deeply wish her to have.

None of the others in this area lead solitary lives, none spend days and nights alone, as Penelope does.

Uncertainty

NOVEMBER 24

I have not seen Penelope for a month. I anticipated that she might withdraw with the onset of mating season and I have noticed the disruption in the behavior patterns of the other deer in the area, yet certain of them have been showing up each day. I have been rising every morning before dawn and going outside in hope of finding Penelope waiting in the dark.

Mid-morning, I put apple pieces in a plastic bag, crossed the road, and clambered down the embankment to the woods in search of any sign of her. There was frost last night, the first of the season, and I guessed that the tick population might have gone dormant. I walked through the woods along the stream, following the pathways made by the deer. Turning to look up, I saw the house as it appears to Penelope. It seemed like a different place, simply for changing perspective. Making my way through the thorns and the other vegetation, I found cloven tracks in the mud beside the water, clear and recent, and thought that I would recognize Penelope's prints by the irregularity of her gait

Paul Bochner

and the impression of her folded foot, if they were present, but I did not see them. I walked for an hour before climbing toward the road and heading home.

If I could see Penelope in the woods or drinking from the stream, even at a distance, it would bring me peace to know that she is alive and is not suffering.

NOVEMBER 30

Over millennia, people have waited in states of uncertainty, lived with denial and hope, for the return of loved ones missing, possibly lost at sea or in battle, presumed injured or incapacitated but still surviving. Such states of anticipation were common and could extend for years. We accept now that information is available and quickly received, no matter how distant the circumstance that may keep someone from returning.

A memory from September 11, 2001, is close at hand. When the planes hit and the towers fell, I was a few miles away, at home, and I felt an incompletion at not having been present. For all any of us knew, there were still thousands of people buried alive and the following morning I drove into the city to volunteer for search and rescue at Ground Zero. Volunteers were being accepted at the Jacob Javits Center until six thirty in the morning. It was not easy getting downtown; the West Side Highway was closed, and Broadway was slow. I arrived at seven, only to find that I was late.

The next morning, I again tried to get there by six thirty and was again a few minutes too late.

In the midst of local, national, global shock suffused with sorrow and grief for thousands dead, my father, on being told that I had tried to volunteer for search and rescue, had only one question, his first, instant words—"Did they reject you?"—not trying to conceal his pleasure at the notion. It is an odd reflexive response to a son in a moment of collective tragedy, but it is a question that a speech-gifted doe might ask a cast-off fawn, a question Penelope's mother

I thought of her each day during the period of separation and sometimes dreamed of her at night.

might ask her. My own mother had repeatedly said to me, "When you were born, your father took one look at you and wanted to send you back," a sentiment now being projected onto others. Yet I may have found some of my strength in this, not paradoxically but linearly, and perhaps Penelope's strength in surviving came similarly. I don't have to search to find congruencies between her early life and my own, and on the chilly evening when I first reached out to her, literally and emotionally, in my offer to care for her, what was being conveyed and what did she know? A few months later, on the August day when she in turn reached out to me, what bond did we recognize?

I am always aware that Penelope is in the world, whether we are together or apart. In the hard rain I worry for her. On a sunny morning, I hope that she is enjoying it. It has been five weeks since I have seen her. With each day I feel less assurance that she is nearby. Almost certainly she is not living in the woods by the lake and simply neglecting to come to the door, or I would have seen her, by herself or with the others, would have glimpsed her at least once in the past weeks. I want her touch, much the same as missing a woman, yet distinct, for in the uncertain absence of a lover there is the pain of intention, of something long or recently cherished which has turned, a wound inflicted, a drifting alienation, rash words spoken which have not been forgiven and will not be forgotten. If Penelope no longer comes, it is not the result of lost love but of something else, simpler or more complex.

I allow myself to imagine her strengthened by a good summer, can see her eating fresh oak and maple leaves, sleeping comfortably in thick piles of them. I hope she will emerge from the woods this evening, tomorrow, soon.

DECEMBER 6

This morning, as the first light was emerging through fog, I looked out and saw Penelope. More than a month had passed since we had seen one another. She came straight to me and took my fingers in her mouth, our reconnection immediate and complete, as if we hadn't been apart for a day.

She has survived a year and a half. The malnourishment and seeming fear that emanated from her late last winter are nowhere in evidence. I clearly remember feeling on that March night that she was near death, and the contrast between then and now is extreme. She does not seem to be in pain. She has put on weight and has grown a thick winter coat. If she no longer needs me as intensely as she did, if I have contributed to her independence, her well-being is my reward.

I am in the unusual situation of being invested in the protection of another life while being largely unable to protect that life. Penelope lives wild and free, and each time she leaves I must trust in her instincts and her good fortune to keep her from harm.

Human / Animal

The word "humanity" is generally defined as "the quality or state of being human." But there follows a second definition: "The quality or state of being kind to other people or to animals," which is contradicted by a third definition: "All people." I try to conjure a world where "all people" are "kind to other people or to animals," and I fail.

"Animality" can be defined as "a quality of nature associated with animals. Vitality. A natural unrestrained, unreasoned response to physical drives or stimuli." This is followed by "the animal nature of human beings." By these definitions, restraint and reason are the distinguishing human characteristics. Yet observing cervine life, I believe that deer live with a higher degree of reason and restraint than most humans. Deer take only what they need to survive and take largely renewable resources. They are not predators and inflict no pain upon creatures of other species, except in extreme situations of self-defense or protection of their young. Moving silently about their terrain in the whisperings of near darkness, they are gentle and nourishing toward their families.

Except when one of them is not. Consider Penelope's mother.

I want to reimagine life in which a disabled fawn would be nurtured and protected by its mother. This desire is one aspect of my own humanity. If there is a circumstance where it is not a feature of animality, it may be due to the imperatives of survival and of evolution. There may be neither restraint nor reason where the survival of a disabled offspring is contemplated. Yet Castle did not kill Penelope when she could easily have done so, and although it took me a long time to realize it, she did not abandon her. As an injured fawn, Penelope was banished, forced to walk away. I have seen its re-enactment and know what that forcing may have looked like, hard hoof strikes to the back, repeated charging, a kick from the mother's strong hind legs, raking swipes to the flesh, all of it repeated until the fawn understood and was gone.

Months after her rejection, when Penelope was a year old, when she had found means of survival without the support or protection of her mother and had endured her early life all alone, when she was still struggling but independent, her mother continued to exhibit violent antipathy toward her. Penelope's mother could not tolerate her disabled fawn. In a confluence of animality with humanity, I placed myself physically in the center of the family, standing between Penelope and her mother, each of us inches apart. Penelope's mother seemed to feel the property was hers, I felt it was mine. Neither of us was wrong; I held legal title to it, which of course meant nothing to Castle. Deer claim territory and, ancestrally, the property might have been in Castle's family for centuries. Yet in this conflict I held a slight edge. Unlike Castle, I could obtain fruit all winter. I had a source of bread and lettuce. I had a pocketknife and hands with which to cut and toss food to those who were hungry on cold nights. While Castle could hiss and snort, I had a strong voice, which I could raise when needed. Castle had sharp hooves and lethally strong legs, but I stood higher and weighed more, so had some intimidating potential and Castle may have known that, had I wanted to, I could have done her harm.

When Penelope sought out her ostracizing family and was repeatedly turned away by her mother, I welcomed her in her family's territory, welcomed her to her birthplace, the place where her mother and siblings spent hours each day. Penelope's siblings did not reject her, yet her mother, nature's designated caregiver and protector, could not abide the sight of her. My own impulses were engaged. The sight of her struggling to survive filled me with a desire to give her comfort, peace, and pleasure. Her health and survival became my goals, an "unrestrained, unreasoned" response to physical drives and stimuli joined with an impulse to be "kind to animals."

Confronting the aggressive mother, I did not think about it in a human way, I acted in an animal way. The survival of the healthy may be a maternal imperative, the rejection and banishment of those not fit for survival an aspect of ensuring survival of the fittest, but because I am not Penelope's biological parent I am free to protect and nurture her for the valuation of life and the cherishment of the living.

And there may be yet another, overlying aspect.

While Penelope has always been apprehensively cautious around humans, at our first contact she allowed me to come within inches of her. She may have sensed in me what I sensed in her, and our connection may have arisen from mutual recognition of inner life. It may seem unlikely that a wild animal and a human could spring from similar, perhaps nearly identical root systems, and even less likely that they could then somehow find each other, but it happened. I believe there is nothing random about this particular animal bonding with this particular human. If she and I could have spoken, we might have sat quietly, shared stories, laughed about it. It might have given her comfort to know that when I told her she was not alone it meant more than I knew. Her childhood and mine held almost surreally comparable elements, many of which I had kept behind a pale scrim of awareness.

We are in the world in similar ways. We have each survived. In this way, we are soul mates. Even without speech and shared stories, she may indeed feel it.

Regarding her as a soul mate, no matter how unconventional, it is important to me to never let her down. Even during times when she does not come every morning, I set the alarm each night, to awaken and be ready to greet her if she should appear. In giving to her, in protecting her, in wanting to see her thrive, I have been given the chance to redress an imbalance. I believe that love is all that matters, the one thing, and that if our lives are bereft of love, no possession, attainment, or reward can compensate or make us whole. A life suffused with love may also be burnished by reward, attainment, and possession but it does not require those to be whole.

I wonder if our capacities for nourishing others are not formed through our own hunger. A particular assertion has come my way over the years from one acquaintance, confirmed in her belief that because I am capable of giving love, I must have received it. "No one," she has said many times, "could be the way you are if they had not had a loving family."

It may be that those who most value freedom are the ones who have been imprisoned. Water may taste best to one who has spent years walking across the desert.

The act of giving holds the power to heal. If it is remarkable, or literally incredible in some eyes, that love can arise spontaneously and not as reflexive continuance of what has been received, it might be more remarkable that a wild animal, wounded, cast off, ostracized and solitary, one whose natural life is familial and communal, should be capable of gestures of affection and gratitude. Three days after Penelope felt safe enough to take food from my fingers, she began to stand with her front feet on my shoes and to lay her head gently against my torso and chest. Her actions seem to be reflections of feeling and an indication that she understands she is loved by me, and that one wild animal has a range of emotions toward one human.

Living surrounded by a variety of humans and deer, Penelope and I have individuated each other. Humans generally agree that deer look much alike, and it may be true that to deer, all humans look quite alike. I have internalized a complex of her features—face, body, markings, movement—which belong solely to Penelope, and I recognize her at a distance or in near darkness. She knows that by coming to the house she will reliably find me, but I have encountered her elsewhere within her range and she has known me out of context, away from the property. One day, driving along this road, I saw her at the southern end of her range, standing at the edge of the pavement, eating grass. I rolled down the window and stopped. She looked at me. I said "Penelle!" my nickname for her, "You know you are not supposed to be on the road. Go over"—meaning the guardrail—"right now." She looked at me a moment longer. "Off the road," I said. And over she went.

She certainly knows my voice. No matter that I wear different clothing from day to day or from one hour to the next, she seems to recognize me. I can go inside for a moment and return having put on a jacket or sweater, which does not negate her visual recognition. It may be that Penelope's sense of smell is sufficient to allow her to know who I am, to distinguish me from my neighbors or from any other person who may be in my house or on my property, without recourse to much visual information. She knows my car and will wait close by as I pull into the driveway and get out. When she is standing safely beside me, she has a startled anxiety reflex when another car pulls into the same driveway. She is afraid of moving vehicles, but not afraid of my moving car. Again, she can predict from past experience that when she sees my car, I will be inside it, that even coming close it will not hit her, that when the door opens it is I who will emerge, and that I will then treat her kindly. This sets aside her fear, and perhaps instills comfort and security. Each of these facets of recognition contains memory which fosters a degree of prediction.

Those who argue that an animal feels no emotion may not have looked clearly at animal life. One basic emotion is fear, and we regularly witness fear in animals responding to our presence by scattering, taking wing, or issuing warnings at our approach. Animals seem to know the length of our reach and how we can move relative to their own range, speed, and ease of escape, which allows them

Her ability to respond to spoken communication feels all the more remarkable because of the innate silence amongst deer.

to choose to strike or to flee from us. Birds know that we cannot fly. Chipmunks know we are too slow to catch them. Fear may be conditioned by similar recognition and predictability in those animals which know we are capable of doing them harm. In related ways, fear may also be an absence of positive prediction born of recognition; the animal is unsure of what we may be capable of and runs. Witness a spider maneuvering to avoid being crushed. If we accept that an animal feels fear, their emotional palette may also reasonably possess other things, to include joy and love.

When Penelope and I saw each other last Sunday, for the first time in more than a month, the fact that she moved directly toward me and took my fingers into her mouth suggests that the time apart did not diminish our bond, did not instill hesitation in her. She retains memory that I have been gentle and protective, knows on sight that she eats from my hand, that I will not hurt her. We each hold knowledge of the other securely within. Her knowledge of me allows her to predict my behavior and provides assurance that I will behave consistently. It did not vanish during our weeks of separation, indicating that the knowledge is internalized and not a reflexive response to momentary circumstance. Equally, my knowledge of her is internalized; I thought of her each day during the period of separation and sometimes dreamed of her at night. Perhaps she dreamed of me. The instant we reconnected we did so on external and internal planes, drawing on shared experience.

DECEMBER 15

It is almost unimaginably warm for mid-December, and I sat outside with coffee and paper as the first light emerged. Looking up, I saw Penelope standing a few feet before me. I brought her apple bowl and she ate several. And after a few moments, from around the other side of the house, there appeared Penelope's family—her mother and the siblings from two generations. Penelope became visibly unsettled; there may have been an earlier altercation. I held out my hands to her in a gesture of reassurance and I told her it was fine, she was with me and I would not let anyone hurt her. Yet she was in the grip of what seemed an adrenaline reaction. She tried to eat but could not continue. She turned and limped away. I went with her a couple of hundred feet onto the vacant neighboring property. Once we were there, Penelope was able to eat a few more apple pieces from my hand. I was again witnessing her banishment, and her knowledge that she is not wanted by her mother. There was nothing to do but stand with her, to let her know that she has me.

DECEMBER 31

While away during the past week, I kept track of the weather in New York to help me imagine how Penelope was doing. This morning, home again, I went outside at 6:30. Through heavy fog I picked out motion hundreds of feet away. As I watched, there emerged the forms of several deer. Ahead of them all, I recognized Penelope's unmistakable, hobbled gait moving toward me. She and I had a joyous reunion. She seemed starved not only for her fruit but for my touch. Gradually the other deer gathered closely and stood watching as Penelope ate from my hands. There were seven of them, not her family but a herd I did not know. As the others gradually moved on, she was aware that they were leaving, yet she chose to remain with me, occasionally turning her head to see where they had gone, and after half an hour she slowly moved in their direction. I saw that she is healthy and that she has been accepted by this new small herd. They each have the same facial proportions—long and narrow, with high-set and dramatically upswept eyes. The matriarch of the herd reminds me of a woman I knew named Renee, and so I named her and her family the Renee herd.

2016

JANUARY 1

Penelope and I celebrated the first morning of the new year with apples and chestnuts. She returned in the evening and after feeding her for a few minutes I noticed that someone else was with her—the same yearling buck she had brought in October, the one I call her boyfriend. He is the only adult male I have seen since November and I was delighted to observe them together. I am deeply hopeful that she is pregnant.

JANUARY 6

For the past week Penelope has been coming every morning, eager for food and physical contact, and she was waiting at six. The temperature with wind chill was in the single digits, yet I felt none of it as we stood together. After a few minutes, from the darkness emerged Penelope's family. For the first time she showed no apparent fear, only a slight unease, at the approach of her mother. We continued with our feeding and when all five had gathered at a distance of fifteen feet, I tossed a few pieces of apple to each of them. Penelope held her ground, standing with me. In a few minutes the circle of family had tightened around us and Penelope was the literal center of attention.

She knows that I feed only her by touch and they have all observed it. This morning, the longer she stood with me, eating from my hand as her mother and siblings watched, the more secure her privileged position seemed. When Penelope let me know that she had eaten enough, the feeding stopped for everyone. As they began to slowly saunter about the yard, I was careful to stay with Penelope, moving in tandem, keeping an eye on her mother. I realized that at that moment I was part of the herd, an effective member of Penelope's family, perhaps the alpha deer, providing food for all, setting down the law to her mother and protecting the most vulnerable member. Penelope gently touched noses with Juno, one of the eight-month-old fawns, her half-sister. While the five moved toward the next property,

Penelope stayed with me. I wanted her to be with her family and after a few minutes she slowly followed them. I don't know what happened once they were out of my range, but this morning felt important. If what is occurring is the reunification of Penelope with her mother, as well as with her half-sisters and -brothers, such has been my goal.

JANUARY 9

This morning Penelope was sleeping a few feet from the door. I stood with her quietly in the darkness, and when eventually she got up, I fed her. After a few minutes her family appeared. Penelope showed no fear and I continued to feed her as the others again gathered in a semi-circle. I tossed apple pieces to everyone while Penelope got the lion's share from my hand. It was the fourth time in a week that the same situation had played out and this morning I felt in Penelope a sense of calm self-possession, as if she and I were jointly hosting breakfast for her family.

JANUARY 10

A dark morning, in several senses; heavy rain was falling as Penelope emerged from the woods. I went out and we stood in the rain as she ate, sharing our private time while everyone else was sleeping. In a while we were again joined by her family, as we had been without incident for the past four days, but today there was backsliding.

Because of the rain, I had kept the small table just inside the door. Needing to get more apples, I backed toward the door, keeping my eye on Castle, standing with her offspring, a few yards from Penelope, who was in her privileged position at the center of the semi-circle. As I got to the door, the instant my back was turned, Castle charged Penelope and she bolted. I went after her, down the embankment and across the road, climbed over the guardrail and toward the stream. There was no reason for me to have abandoned her in that situation. I should have stood with her and driven away the others and I was aching from the mistake I had made. I imagined her own emotions, seeing me leave my post as her guardian, having her mother suddenly take advantage of my absence to threaten her.

Looking through the woods and along the stream I could not see Penelope, who must have been frightened enough to run to a distance. After a series of mornings where she and her family had shared an uneasy truce, Penelope had been chased and I needed to let her know that I was with her. Standing in the rain, I detached and observed myself from somewhere nearby, a man in an unusual situation, holding apples, calling the name of a wild deer, wanting to apologize.

Unable to find her, I finally walked back to the house. Castle, Daisy, and the fawns were still in the yard and I chased Castle away. She had undone the good that had been achieved over the past several days, in one impulsive rush. Penelope had begun to be at ease with her, and I do not know if that level of ease can be regained. The weight of my failure increased through the day. In the afternoon, I was careful to get home to wait for Penelope, needing her to know that I was sorry, that we were okay, that sometimes progress doesn't follow a straight path. She did not appear.

JANUARY 11

This morning, again, Penelope did not come. I should try to remind myself as well that progress doesn't follow a straight path, but I feel I did a terrible and thoughtless thing. I will try hard to never again turn my back on Castle when Penelope is with me.

JANUARY 12

I have not seen Penelope since the incident Sunday morning, and her mother has not come either, after several days where everyone was getting along. It seems that each is aware of the disruption.

Castle learned last winter that my presence signaled apples for her and her twins. She seemed to have been learning that the sight of Penelope standing beside me meant that she and her newer fawns would also be fed. Castle may be able to learn cause and effect, that if she threatens Penelope there will be no feeding, and I will continue to try to teach her.

There are moments when I question whether, by striving to protect Penelope and to regulate the bullying from her mother, trying to integrate her with others of her family and species, I am interfering with the natural order. Yet I am an animal living in the middle of their range, which is also my range. They live here, I live here, as do the birds, insects, various mammals, and other humans. If we project backwards by millennia, this patch of earth was home to much the same array of creatures. They lived side by side, breathing the same air and sharing the same water with each other, feeling the same grass, sand, moss, stones, and mud beneath their feet. Each species impacted the lives of the others. Whether the humans lived in caves or in teepees, they probably hunted the deer more than fed them. And yet, in prehistoric art found at several European sites, deer figure prominently, drawn with fine observation and rendered with respect.

Statistically, the deer's most active predator at present is the automobile. It may be a stretch to view a car as being an element of nature, yet it is an artifact of human evolution, a manifestation of humanity's nature, and therefore an aspect of the natural order. Having replaced spears and arrows with bullets and fast-moving metal boxes which take the deer's lives in massive numbers, we are still their primary predators. There are more than 2.1 million deer-vehicle collisions reported each year in America. Oddly, these are tallied to result in 440 fatalities—the figure represents human fatalities—and there is annually an estimated ten billion dollars in damages—to cars—from striking deer. No word about how many deer fatalities result, the deer not being protected by two tons of steel at the moment of impact, nor how much damage is done to their families, the orphaned fawns, and the mothers left behind.

> *I had stood up for her, almost certainly the first time in her life anyone had chased away an aggressor. And I had done it in the deer's own language.*

Nature's order may be more mutable than we assume, and in continual flux. A shepherd employs dogs to guard his sheep. Not long ago the dog descended from the wolf, which preyed upon the sheep. Wolves gave rise to dogs in an evolutionary branch which did not eliminate the wolf but produced a similar animal characterized by diametrical impulses. The contrast was encouraged and capitalized on by yet another animal: the human shepherd. If human intervention led to the predator's development into the guardian, then the wolf, the sheep, the dog, and the human are equally part of the natural order.

Penelope and the other deer might reasonably regard humans as predators, yet as with the dog emerging from the wolf, at least one human in their range has become their protector. The deer and I seem increasingly at ease within our communal environment. I exult in sharing the property with them. It is mine only in relation to other humans. In relation to all other creatures, it is ours—theirs and mine—and it was theirs long before I arrived. In all probability it will be theirs long after I'm gone. I take measures to ensure their comfort and their survival. I leave dense growth in which mothers hide their new fawns. By raking the autumn leaves into large piles I provide the deer with nests, used by many of them throughout the year, for nighttime sleeping and daytime naps. They also eat the gathered leaves, oak and maple being favored. Giving Penelope modest quantities of other things which are not at present indigenous, but all of which have at times grown here—apples, chestnuts, grapes—is evidently to her pleasure and not to her detriment. If the ancient apple tree were still standing, if the grape vines still produced, if chestnut trees grew here as they grow nearby, she would be eating those things, as she now receives them from me.

Despite her disabled leg, Penelope has become healthy and strong. Her impulse to groom me seems closely related to the behavior between herd-mates. Having been denied her own grooming, she may be expressing gratitude and affection, as acknowledgement that I behave differently from the deer who could have cared for her but instead rejected her. She may see me as a mother figure, or as something different.

The aspect of our physical contact that appears to be unique, separate from the deer's shared physicality, is Penelope's taking my fingers into her mouth and holding them there each time we approach one another. For me, in that first touch, my hand held by her, she and I are together again and any pain or anxiety I have felt during our separation evaporates. She lingers, postponing feeding, holding me as long as she can. Animals know the imperatives of connection. Watching the joy of a dog reunited with its master, we see that it is not enough to greet the dog verbally, not enough to offer food. The dog demands touching of a specific kind, degree, and duration; barking, crying, wagging, and dancing to receive appropriate response before the reunion can feel complete. For Penelope also, our private rituals of reconnection seem vital.

JANUARY 15

Wednesday evening, minutes before darkness, Penelope's attention was suddenly riveted by something I could not see. She stopped eating and stared at a stand of dense spruce a few yards from where we stood. I walked toward the trees, seeing nothing, but following her focus, I gradually made out the fragmentary form of a deer, standing behind the low branches, staring at us. Although I could not clearly see the deer's head or body, I spotted the unique foot markings of Penelope's mother. Castle and I have had a bad week. After having been tolerant of Penelope for several days, she reverted in a moment of hostility and I have not acknowledged her since. Now she was hiding, watching us. I took several firm steps toward her hiding place and she bolted.

Even as Penelope is now more than a year and a half old, the tensions between her and Castle persist. Her fear of her mother is built on experience. But Castle's animosity toward Penelope, her continued impulse to drive her away, is mysterious. I wonder where it resides in a mother, the chronic and sustained rejection of an offspring. Given that Penelope was born whole, that she was injured while still a few weeks old, her mother's animus toward her was acquired at the same time Penelope became disabled. Forced to fend for herself against substantial odds, she endured last year's brutal winter alone. She was not nursed or protected as her siblings have been and this fact renders her more equipped for survival than they, rather than less. It may be a refined survival skill to have found me, to accept my invitation, to stay close, and to come for daily feedings.

If a parent's instinctual nurturance of an offspring can be altered by circumstance, as it was altered in one direction by Penelope's injury, can it be altered again in a different direction, regained or resurrected, by her survival? Can it be altered by the advocacy of a loving partner, even one of another species, altered by inducement and enticement? Can my ability to give and withhold encourage Castle to do as I wish, to accept the one who has for so long been an outcast? For reasons large and small, it matters to me that Penelope be given her best chance.

JANUARY 17

Deer play games all their lives. At dusk, they can be seen in the woods, down by the pond, running, chasing, and leaping, making swift reversals, figure eights and feints to surprise their playmates, splashing through the water, over and again.

Penelope cannot do that, but she devises games for us. In a new elaboration, she tries to go around me while I am cutting her apples, to take them whole, directly from the table. This makes me laugh, not only because it is a variation, but because, due to a deer's incomplete dentition, she is incapable of picking up the apples and simply succeeds in nudging them off the table and onto the ground. Like all deer, she has six lower front incisors and two canines, a gummy plate on the top, no teeth in the middle of upper or lower jaw, and large, strong molars in back, which serve her herbivorous foraging. I have spent a great deal of time with my fingers inside Penelope's mouth and know the feel of the ridged roof, her teeth and gums, the broad tongue, and agile, soft lips. Receiving food from me, sharing our eating rituals and her invented games, she evidently enjoys the entire sequence, including my laughter, and it seems clear, from the repetitions and the variations she devises, that she knows when a game is comical. If, as a joke, I extend a whole apple toward her, she seems to recognize the humor. Playing along, she gamely tries to take a bite, her lips, gums, and lower teeth make a squeaking sound against the skin of the apple without breaking it or taking it and after a couple of tries she gives up, knowing I will cut it properly and feed her the pieces.

JANUARY 18

The mystery of what could have caused the open wound, which Penelope had on her right flank when first she came to me, may now be solved. Last evening, the nearest neighbors, Barbara and Frank, pulled into their driveway, about one hundred feet from where Penelope and I stood. They are gentle and quiet people and Penelope has never shown any stress at their presence. Yet last night something was alerting her; she stopped eating and stared in their direction. They were carrying their skis and poles from the car to the house. She bolted in terrified flight, moving quickly. I called to her and went after her. Hyperventilating, she stopped, never taking her eyes from the direction of the neighbors' driveway. I was unable to comfort her and she continued toward the woods.

The only difference between normal circumstance and yesterday's was Frank and Barbara carrying their skis and poles, a sight which scared Penelope so much that she ran from me while being fed. If the weapon which had pierced her had been bow and arrow, and not a BB or pellet gun, as I thought possible, and if Penelope had observed her assailant prepare and raise it, the shape of the skis, with their curved ends, might reasonably have reminded her of the bow and the slender, straight poles of the arrows.

I believe it triggered a memory of the moment she had received her wound. If the arrow had lodged within her flank, the shaft broken off, it would have resulted in the mass with its open, running center. I can't find another explanation. If correct, she has for a year carried the memory of a sequence of sensations and of deliberately inflicted suffering.

She may also have learned from the event which caused her primary disability. She is wary of cars. This morning after her apples and chestnuts, she went to the edge of the property, looking across the road to where Renee's family stood. They were all staring at Penelope, seeing her standing on what they seem to regard as her own property. She clearly wanted to join the other deer.

A steady, intermittent stream of cars was passing at moderate speed, yet posing a lethal threat should she emerge onto the road. I silently thought, "let them come to you. Please don't cross." Penelope always waits, looks both ways, and listens. This morning, she waited, and when there was a long, clear moment, she went down the embankment, slipped across the road and over the guardrail to join her new group. Her caution may be the result of innate intelligence, but if, as I suspect, her leg injury was the result of being swiped by a car, she must also carry a memory of that incident.

She exhibits a well-developed awareness of cause and effect; one thing will perhaps or probably lead to another. When I pick up the small wooden table on which I cut her apples, and carry it outside, she licks her lips and wags her tail. The table signifies food to her because its appearance presages a sequence of events and to encourage that expectation of constancy I have tried to never betray her anticipation.

Penelope's ease has developed as the result of an accumulation of experience which engenders knowledge of me as an individual and does not expand or generalize to include other humans. With the singular exception of last night's fear of Frank and Barbara, at any given moment, in response to other people, when she is uneasy she stays beside me and allows me to touch her.

Penelope lives in her natural habitat, comes when she wishes, and, as happened in the fall, she can stay away for weeks and return when ready. As I anticipated in September, with the arrival of her first mating season her focus was on her own kind, a life force apparently undiminished by having formed her bond with me. The things we have learned together have not reduced her capacity to live as she had before we connected and seemingly have not altered her nature. They may have given her an alternative mode of being in her world, the way a person can possess two or more modes of behavior, to be activated in varying circumstances. Living freely in the woods, she adapted her touching and grooming instincts, when they were denied her, by applying them to me, without becoming domesticated. While she may now regard me as a sort of mate, she knew that I was not a deer and that my suitability as a substitute had to be tested. Her testing phase lasted as long as she needed it to and changed when she was ready to allow it to progress. She decided precisely when the tests had been passed, and she knew which things might then proceed and be accepted. She may have been imagining them in anticipation.

Penelope

JANUARY 25

The heavy snow which fell over the past weekend was characterized as a "historic blizzard." I was worried for Penelope when I fed her on Friday night. She did not show at all on Saturday, with conditions at their worst. I had been watching for her yesterday and had all but given up when, just as darkness fell, I went outside for one last look. She was standing in high snow, beside a row of spruce trees, a dark shape against darker shapes, almost invisible. It was difficult for her to move through the deep snow and I went to her, making several trips, bringing her warm chestnuts and fruit, standing with her while she ate, knowing she had already had a hard couple of days.

She finally trudged into the darkness to sleep in the snow, most likely alone. Despite her connections with Renee's family, and her easier position in relation to her own family, Penelope is still substantially solitary. I sense this from her comings and goings, the times I have seen her in the woods near the house and elsewhere in her range. None of the others in this area lead solitary lives, none spend days and nights alone, as Penelope does. Last evening, standing together in the falling snow, I had done what I could, had fed her well, had stroked her, had spoken to her in a gentle voice. We live in different, if overlapping, worlds, yet the desire for another to be spared suffering is an indivisible aspect of love.

FEBRUARY 2

Preparing chestnuts for Penelope every morning, cooking them at the same time I make coffee, I have understood that she wants the water in which the nuts have been boiled. She now gets twenty or thirty in a bowl with the warm, infused water. As the seasonal supply of fresh chestnuts vanishes by January, I have found a chestnut farm in Washington State that offers them dried and I order thirty pounds at a time, which I rehydrate each day as needed. Thirty pounds of dried is equivalent to ninety pounds of fresh and makes quite a bit of soup. The woman who takes my orders said she had never heard of anyone buying them for a deer—they do everything possible to fence out the deer on their farm—but a sale is a sale, and it is a perfect arrangement.

This morning, after she had eaten all she could, Penelope groomed me for ten minutes, then licked the sleeves of my woolen sweater, which may feel somewhat like a deer body, and invited me to groom her at the same time. She is increasingly at ease, whether she has me to herself or whether there are other deer present. There has been no aggression from her mother for a while. Castle can stand five feet from Penelope, taking the few pieces of apple I toss her, watching Penelope receiving privileged treatment. When other deer come around, Penelope stays with me, knowing that even though I will offer them some food, she is the only one to be touched and fed by hand. She knows I am hers, and by giving food to the others we are extending a peace offering.

Hollywood meets Penelope

FEBRUARY 10

A car stopped on the road this morning, an unusual sight, as this is a narrow road with no shoulder. I went out, walked to the edge of the property and looked down. A man was standing beside the car, looking up at the house. "Everything okay?" I asked. "Yes, sure, fine," he replied. "I'm scouting locations."

I invited him up, he introduced himself as Robert Noonan and told me he was the location scout for a forthcoming feature film to be directed by Todd Haynes. Haynes's currently-released film, *Carol*, starring Cate Blanchett and Rooney Mara, is at the moment nominated for six Oscars. Robert told me that the new project, titled *Wonderstruck*, takes place in two periods, fifty years apart. One half of the film is set in a specific sort of house in Minnesota; he was searching for the right house and had just passed mine. I asked when they were planning to shoot. When he answered the spring, I told him that I could not allow shooting from mid-May until mid-June. "I have a deer," I told him. "She'll be ready to give birth around the last week in May. I need this place to be completely quiet and safe for her to have her baby." To convey that I am not totally insane, I showed him a couple of videos of Penelope and briefly sketched her story. He asked if he could take photographs of the exterior of the house and property, and whether he could come another day to shoot the interiors.

FEBRUARY 12

Returning today, Robert's first questions concerned "the deer situation." I showed him the area that I consider their sanctuary and explained that I leave it untouched, rarely setting foot there. I pointed out the small patch where, each year, fawns are born, and I told him that Penelope had been born there and would probably want to give birth to her own fawn in the same spot. He understood and kindly reminded me that were the interiors to be used for shooting, the exterior would be ringed with lighting, directed through the windows. I explained my commitment, that Penelope's well-being and her safety matter more to me than any other consideration. When he mentioned money, I told him that no matter how much they might offer, I would not let anything interfere with the birth of her baby.

"What if we plan around Penelope's pregnancy?" Robert asked. "Suppose we were to come the end of June?" Wanting to be polite, I told him that it might work out, imagining the item in Variety: "Cast and Crew Await Birth of Fawn." The cast, including Julianne Moore and Michelle Williams, would have been waiting for a disabled, abandoned, and cherished deer, which felt like a slightly ironic yet fitting priority, although in my heart I couldn't imagine allowing such an invasion of Penelope's world. Without giving an outright no, I told him that I would be relieved if they chose another house.

When Robert finished shooting stills of the interior, we walked outside. Penelope rarely comes at noon, yet here she was, as if on cue, to support the unlikely story I had told. As soon as she saw an unfamiliar person with me, she stopped at the edge of the property.

I went to her and fed her chestnuts while at a distance Robert took a few photos of her and of the two of us together. I pointed out her apprehension in the presence of a single unknown person and said, "Imagine a whole film crew."

As soon as Robert drove away, Penelope walked with me to the door. The fear and consternation she would experience seeing sixty or more people swarming the house and property, the trucks, lights, and noise, day after day for weeks; she would think that everything she had come to accept had ended. I would not even have been here to try to reassure her.

Her life has been shaped by fear and displacement. Although the other deer in the area are kinder to her now, she still goes off most evenings into the darkness to spend the night alone. In the morning, the first thing she does upon waking is come to me. Much of my joy at the thought of her pregnancy comes from knowing that she will no longer be solitary, that with a fawn of her own she will have another soul that is hers, beside her constantly, for a year at a minimum. If her fawn is female, they might stay together for life. Castle is still bound to Daisy, and to the more recent twin fawns she delivered last spring. The four move as a family. A fawn of Penelope's will also be a genetic part of Castle's family, and I can't predict how that dynamic might play out.

For these reasons and more, the arrival of this fawn is to be protected and celebrated. I hope that if and when she is ready to give birth, Penelope will see this property as her haven, that she will hide her fawn here in its first weeks and will know that I am watching over them both. I am responsible to speak for her, and I turned down the production company's request to shoot here.

Ironically, when Penelope first came into my life, and her very survival seemed unlikely, my friend Carol said, "I think she'll have a baby." It was an extremely improbable event, but I promised I would name the baby after her—Carol for a girl, Carroll for a boy. And so, in the strangeness of life, Penelope's nascent fawn will have the same name as Mr. Haynes's currently Oscar-nominated film.

Home to many

One of the joys of living surrounded by nature is to observe how many individual organisms thrive on this small patch of earth. The largest are the mature trees, which number almost one hundred: spruce, pine, oak, maple, cherry, poplar, dogwood, birch. Engaging in vigorous cycles of reproduction, every spring the maples send down many thousands of twirling seed pods, each a marvel of functional design, and many of them secure a hold in the earth. The oaks drop thousands of acorns. Thumb-sized evergreens show themselves everywhere and if left undisturbed grow at the rate of about a foot per year. I have transplanted small spruce, to give them a better chance, and in so doing have been forced to mark the passage of time by their current heights. A six-inch tree can become a twenty-footer while we are focused elsewhere, and if in an unexpected moment its size is noticed, I ponder where the time has gone.

Animals dwell within as well as on the trees. Which mammals consider the trees to be their home? How many varieties of birds? From time to time a nest will become visible, or fall to the earth in heavy wind, and there are many others so well constructed and camouflaged that they must remain hidden indefinitely. Underground, what mazes and tunnels run? Digging a couple of inches into one of the compost piles exposes multitudes of worms. One day a star-nosed mole surfaced, somehow, inside the sunroom, one of the oddest creatures I had ever seen, and I scooped it up and took it outside.

Chipmunks have their own pieces of sub-real estate, making large, elaborate single-occupancy burrows, with multiple entrances, individual rooms for food storage, hygiene, and sleeping and drainage in the floors.

One night, hearing an unfamiliar sound in the kitchen, I discovered a flying squirrel sitting on the breakfast table. Countless mice have visited and occupied the house for varying stints. Birds of various sizes and colors have come down the chimney and I have helped them exit through an open window or door. One morning an exotic duck, having veered off course, was waddling around the living room. In the yard, skunks, raccoons, and possums used to be

frequent sights in near darkness, yet for unknown reasons they have become rarities. In summer, bats dart in the humid dusk, eating mosquitoes, which certainly thrive. Fireflies, crickets, dragonflies abound. Wasps nest in the trees and sometimes in the eaves and crawlspaces. Wild turkeys saunter through the yard from time to time and a few have decided to make this their home, staying for long periods. One day a large snapping turtle navigated the driveway, evidently moving from the stream to the lake, very slowly and quite some distance, and I can't comprehend how the turtle knew the lake was there.

If it were possible to pay equal attention to all the varieties of life, to recognize the squirrels and doves individually, to name them, what relationships, what traits of humor, shyness, ingenuity, or aggression, what dramas of love and conflict, might be revealed? For decades I observed deer as an undifferentiated mass. To know them as individuals, I simply needed to look.

FEBRUARY 19

By looking through the windows, Penelope searches for me inside the house. If she can't see me in one window she moves to the next, knowing that upon spotting her I will come out. She knows that not only do I live both outside and inside, but that Monkey does. Monkey is a member of the animal world who also gets fed by me, gets carried, gets to lie in the hammock, ride in the car, and enter the house when it is dark or cold. Penelope sees that Monkey later emerges from the house and that nothing has happened to her. I am guessing that we are heading for the time when Penelope will feel comfortable coming into the house, perhaps to shelter from the rain as she now shelters under the dense evergreens. If she continues to thrive in her natural environment, it will take nothing from her. In ways that none of the other deer have, she has struggled with physical pain, and with rejection, aggression, and solitude. All of these might have led to her failure to thrive and to her death. But she is a fighter, and she accepts the support I offer as an asset, an adjunct to her strength. She needs to survive as a wild deer and to live among her own kind, for as long as she is capable, and if indeed she gives birth in the spring it will be important that she raise her fawn to live in the wild. Yet there is nothing to be proven or gained by further suffering, and it is right that she receives extra privileges.

FEBRUARY 22

I hadn't seen the Renee herd for a couple of weeks and assumed they had moved on, but last night Penelope and I were joined by four of them. They may have had a reason to follow her here, from observing that she knows where to find good food or because she communicated with them in some way as to where she was headed. I tossed many pieces of apple to them, their reward for being kind to Penelope, as they watched her being lavishly fed. One by one, they drifted away while she was still eating and Penelope was visibly conflicted between staying with me or going with them. After she had eaten a sufficient amount I encouraged her to go, leading her a few steps until she walked purposefully in the direction they had gone, toward the lake. It was a moment of happiness near the end of a gentle day. Penelope had health, freedom from pain, and the companionship of other deer.

She returned this morning, alone, from the other direction. Whether she had gone off to spend the night by herself or had just been wandering for a while at dawn I don't know. I was waiting for her and we had an hour together with warm chestnut soup and her favorite apples. As the sun rose, she walked away in the same direction she had last night, perhaps to join Renee and her family. I will be curious to see whether they follow her here again at dusk.

FEBRUARY 23

Indeed, yesterday evening, Penelope was with seven from the Renee herd. While they all watched from fifteen or twenty feet, Penelope received her chestnuts and Honeycrisp apples. And as I was cutting her second apple, I also tossed pieces to the nearby deer. She got her soup, the others again seeing the odd sight of one of their number drinking from a ceramic bowl held for her at mouth level, then effusively grooming the hands, wrists and wool-clad arms of the person who was feeding her, and I try to imagine what they think at the sight of a deer having a close relationship with a human. They see that she is stroked and petted, that I speak to her in a conversational tone, a stream of sounds which, for all they know, she understands, and she does understand much of it.

I want to encourage them to see her as the source of goodness and privilege. The double-tiered feeding had its intended effect. The others stayed at a modest distance. They maintained their focus on Penelope, and I rewarded them, making sure everyone got a share of the apples. My own reward was seeing Penelope leave with the herd for the second evening in a row. Wishing to ease her solitude, I find signs that it is happening.

FEBRUARY 24

Comparing Penelope's face to any of the others, in or out of her family, there is a vivid distinction. While each of the other deer appear in degrees somewhat rough, wild, uncertain, Penelope looks the way a person does when she knows she is loved. She has gained a refinement, a directness in her eyes, and she has become serenely beautiful. It is evident in photos of her, and several people have remarked on it, unprompted, noting how different from other deer her facial aspect appears. To see this serenity in the face of a wild animal, and to know that there is every reason for it, is a reflection of the changes in her inner life.

Penelope's resilience calls into question the biblical phrase "the meek shall inherit the Earth." The idea may have been based on nothing more than hopeful and defensive thinking, certainly not on historical observation. The meek are crushed, driven out, overrun, stolen from, mutilated, raped, starved, and killed by the millions. They may inherit a graceful afterlife but this Earth is not inherited, it is taken by those who are least meek. The endless proofs comprise so much of our education and our entertainment, the strong vanquishing those weaker, the greedy taking from the needy, cruelty overcoming kindness.

Penelope is not one of the strong. If she seems to be laying claim to this piece of the Earth, it is not by virtue of her gentility but because she has gained the devotion of a strong ally. Almost one year ago I committed myself to Penelope's well-being and to her survival. I have stood beside her and stood between her and her enemies. It would not have sufficed to protect her in a single instance, not enough to give her the equivalent of a pep talk, as some bullied children are given, about not allowing herself to be mistreated. It is not enough to tell a victim to stand up for themselves, they must be stood up for.

Taking the position of her defender, I followed through every time I saw her threatened. The signal was received by her mother, and by others, that Penelope was no longer alone, that she and I were a team. I have no way to know how such knowledge was processed and transformed into a degree of her own courage, but there were times when it was almost palpable.

In storytelling, the meek who become vanquishers do so by literal transformation. Peter Parker, Clark Kent, Tony Stark, and the many other heroes whose fictions abound must be transformed in measurable and graphic ways into Spiderman, Superman, Ironman, before their process of inheritance commences. And if, as the tagline would have it, "with great power comes great responsibility," perhaps it is true that any strength carries with it some responsibility, not to enact its own needs but to provide for the needs of those lacking in strength. Aspects of morality demand the extension of strength to cover the weak.

The joy I take in seeing Penelope thrive is enhanced by having enabled her. In a similar way, when I read a positive review of the work of someone who has devoted themselves to their art and their craft, I am thrilled for them, whether they are strangers or whether, as happens, I have supported them. I imagine what they may be feeling in reading appreciation for their writing, painting, acting, academic advancement, scientific research. Life and work are hard and almost anyone who thrives does so by virtue of the struggle and the failures that have preceded their success. For many years I have devoted a portion of my time to helping others with their work. I am sent a broad range of material with the request that I edit, amend, suggest. I take seriously the requests of those who take their own work seriously. I never shrug it off with a facile "Great, I loved it," because to do so would be disrespectful.

The years I have spent pursuing my own visions in solitude have taught me that when left alone we can easily lose sight of our direction and purpose. Solitude may be common, can become a temperamental imperative, but it is, I feel, against nature. Watching

Paul Bochner

What draws us toward another life? It may be a desire for completion. It may be a form of self-recognition.

Penelope living alone while the area is replete with other deer, many of them related to her, all of whom live communally, I believe that her abandonment and her banishment from the family forced a solitary identity upon her. Penelope's life exists outside her family, and even though she is accepted by Renee's herd, she leaves them after a time to be by herself.

It is important to me that she knows I will be here when she comes, yet I too am a transitory part of her day. She may stay with me for an hour or two and then move on. It may be that whatever one's social identity, it is set early and may be immune to change or may change only with sustained effort. Having lived in a community, having known and observed individuals for decades, it is striking how consistently their social states remain unchanged. There are those who can be considered chronic isolates, people whom I have never once seen engaged in conversation with another person, those I have seen wandering alone at night in a manner that conveys no one awaiting their return or arrival, in the same way they wandered thirty years earlier. Those who may, through death, divorce, or other separation, have lost families or partners, will often find or create other partnerships or families, their identity being connective. Most of the people I know exist in a sustaining state, whether of connection or isolation.

Many who are in search of change, who lack partnership yet desire it, those who approach another in an expressed search for love and oneness, will swiftly or ultimately move on in their own ways. Some choose solitude, even when acknowledging that they have finally received the love and companionship they sought. They will find a reason, often small, perhaps constructed or invented, to justify their eventual self-exile. Maybe the search itself has been their identifying state and in order to be true to their nature, in order that their identity be sustained, they must keep searching. I wonder whether Penelope's identity as a solitary creature might have been open to change when she was in the first months of her life and came back to the property, apparently hoping to rejoin her mother, sister, and brother. Had she not been chased

It may be incorrect to think that I have achieved anything with her, more correct to see that she tamed me, showed me what she wanted me to know, led me to give her what she hoped to receive.

away, had she been allowed to remain, could she have overcome the early banishment and isolation to accept the identity of a deer living with her family?

I wonder whether her foundational identity as an isolate may eventually cause her to leave me, to resume her solitary life.

Even among the deer whose fawns are healthy, I sometimes see mothers competing with their offspring for food, not just in the deprivations of winter but when there is ample for all. My dedication to Penelope's well-being comes before my own in several ways, none of which feel to be hardship, all of which bring me fulfillment. Even when the night has been hard and sleep brief, I awaken at dawn to be ready to greet her. I rush home in late afternoon to be here when she arrives. I have not counted how much I spend for her food; I would happily go without if it meant providing for her.

The least happy people I know are those whose lives reflect mostly upon themselves. The happiest I know are those who have a consuming interest and outward focus. Their individual lives are in every sense enriched by addressing and merging with the larger world, whether it be animal, botanical, astronomical, philosophical, theoretical. In a universe, in a town, in a back yard, with questions to be considered and shared, when there are multitudes of lives in so many forms, in motion all around us, brimming with mystery, when our planet is a fragment of even that which we know to exist, let alone what we can only sense or presume—with all that, let's talk about "me?"

From cradle to grave, many people are cruelly imprisoned by their own viewpoint, locked into seeing the world through their own eyes, which keeps them from broader and greater experience. Perhaps such imprisonment does worse, diminishing them in an intensifying spiral; the more they feel "me-me-me" the poorer they become,

increasing their dissatisfaction, which causes them to focus on their own lives and on how they feel about themselves. It may be equally true that the more we focus elsewhere, the happiness and liberty so gained free us to further let go of the self-confinement, the "me-me-me" voice, and open ourselves to the experiences of other lives.

The moment Penelope appears, I am relieved, and the word "relief" carries multiple meanings. She relieves me of my own burdens. If I awaken on a given morning to thoughts of self, to remorse or self-recrimination, the instant I begin to care for her my thoughts are directed toward her and away from myself. Giving her the touch of my hand or the taste of chestnuts, seeing her pleasure, I am filled with pleasure inseparable from hers. By letting go of my aspect of the moment, by entering as much as possible into her aspect, I feel ecstasy; literally, being outside myself.

The unification of lives may be an ideal voiced in song, spoken at weddings, whispered at graveside while we weep over what we have lost through the separations of death, but I think the experience of unification is rare. To become "we" with another life, to experience love, separate from and above our own momentary sensations, requires a willing self-negation. "Negation" inescapably carries negative connotations, but used in this sense, it is productive. Self-negation extends us. It expands the self.

Maybe the elusive definition of love comes a step closer when we cease to think of it as involving two parties and think of a single party, atomized only for purposes of identification. If I awaken to a thunderstorm, my first thought is to hope that Penelope is safe. Of an early morning, if she appears before I have had one sip of coffee, I go to her and place warm soup on her wooden table. I stand in the cold or the rain if she is standing in cold or rain, and I feel no hunger, thirst, cold, or wetness. I feel the satisfaction that she is eating when hungry, that she is getting what she enjoys the most. Love is embodied in every part of the process. It exists in the connection, even when she and I are miles apart. Many people know that my love of Penelope has become one of the biggest parts of who I am, and they ask about her

before asking how I am. In answering, I am suffused with the oneness of self-negation, filled with joy to share any aspect of her life.

FEBRUARY 29

Last night's Oscar telecast ran well past midnight. I slept briefly, and although I was tired, leapt out of bed in the dark so that I would be ready to take care of Penelope. While watching others acknowledged for their work, I was thrilled when someone whose talent I admire was called, when they spoke to accept praise. When an honoree expressed gratitude and love to colleagues, partners, or parents, I felt joy for those being thanked.

Once the boundaries of self are dissolved it matters less who is being celebrated than that a celebration is occurring. Those who report a sense of hollowness even in the face of receiving rewards may be revealing a greater truth than the simple idea that reward, by itself, is hollow. Recognition, fame, or wealth may bring no satisfaction when their end point is only self. "Me" is, by definition, an isolating imprisonment by force of boundaries. Letting go of "me," the pleasures can become literally boundless, because we are all freed to enjoy the success of another, to enjoy anyone's success, to feel triumph in every nomination and every golden statuette. No individual has won, no one has taken anything from anyone else, because in that moment there is no you or me, there is us. On the rare occasion I watch any athletic event I feel good for every athlete, applaud every play that has been well made, each score, no matter what team the player is on, no matter who is winning. Someone has made a good throw, a good catch, sunk a basket or a putt, kicked the ball through the goal, hit one over the fence, crossed home plate, and I am happy for them. Being on both teams at once, there is only victory.

It is sport, however, and not a political contest with actual consequence. It is not war where survival is at stake. Not a court case where someone's life or freedom hang on the verdict. It is not a situation of scarcity, where there is a limited amount of clean water and seeing that water flow to others and not to oneself or to one's family means death. Yet accounts of life-or-death scarcity often reveal a sobering capacity to share, to ensure the survival of all. The trapped Chilean miners, who had no idea how long they would be underground or whether they would ever be freed, had minuscule amounts of water and food, yet they shared with each other, showing unimaginable restraint, taking a single bite or drop on the tongue before passing what they had to the next man.

Being given an award in the arts is generally a reflection of skill, talent, insight, perhaps a measure of how much one has offered and given to others, even if the gift is only a kind of aspirational glamour. It is unlikely that the bestowing of an Oscar will cause mass starvation, infringement of human rights, genocide, border hostilities. Life will continue much the same for almost everyone, save perhaps the nominal recipient, whose fortunes may surge or decline, having attained a theoretical high point. Those who most easily thrive in the wake of winning are those who will thrive whether they win or not.

Freedom through self-negation can be the straightest path toward love, and toward happiness. Seeing Penelope thrive helps me to thrive. The more fully I remove any separation between her and myself, the greater our joy. I have transformed toward this position through experience, the only teacher I trust. I don't think we can be deliberately taught any of these things. Maybe we cannot even hear them.

There are other people who have earned the trust of wild animals, have nurtured them, enabled their survival, protected them or their environments and brought them to health without removing them from their habitat. I'm guessing that each of these people also learned by doing, Jane Goodall, in her connection to wild chimpanzees, being a glowing example. Another is Joe Hutto, who has lived in Montana among the wild mule deer. A documentary about him chronicles the two years of daily presence it took before the herd began to allow him to get close.

Penelope allowed me to get within touching distance almost immediately. She was the one doing the leading, making the decisions, setting the timeframe. It may be incorrect to think that I achieved anything with her, more correct to see that she tamed me, showed me what she wanted me to know, led me to give her what she hoped to receive. She figured it out by herself, day by day, and maybe she is as pleased and as amazed as I am by the relationship we developed, proud that she taught a human her signals.

MARCH 2

Penelope owns little. She has me and has entitlement to what I can share with her—home and food. She may also have a couple of nests which are, by moral right, her own real estate. I have a rough idea of their locations: one in the woods by the stream, the other down by the lake. Penelope possesses her intrinsic strengths. She has the growing respect and acknowledgement of the other deer. She has the extended affection of many people who know about her and take an interest in her and in her well-being. Those intangible assets are real; they may be worth more in the short and long terms that anything that can be lost, stolen, sold, bought, taxed, or repossessed. Yet Penelope will not inherit the world. Her powers, even of self-protection, are limited. The world of her ancestors—and the fossil record shows that whitetail deer have flourished as a species for millions of years—offered them cleaner air, cleaner water, had no murderous vehicles to mow them down at high speed. Whatever plants Penelope finds to eat are probably in diminished supply and variety compared to what was available on this piece of land in earlier centuries.

The deer do not have many friends, and most people would not place Penelope's well-being above their own. There are periodic calls to cull the deer population, "cull" being a polite word for kill. They are vilified for eating cultivated as well as native plants, deemed a suburban nuisance in the way that rats are unwanted in cities, and they are poisoned, their extermination seen as desirable. They are blamed rather than pitied for the large number of deer-automobile collisions.

    I do place Penelope's well-being above my own. My efforts to protect her may not be enough to ensure that she lives a full life. I live with anxiety that she will be harmed, injured, or killed, and I am largely powerless to prevent any of those from occurring. She may, for a time and through my intervention, inherit some place on this earth, but she and those like her will probably not prevail in any human sense, their habitat encroached upon even as the whitetail population is counted as growing out of bounds.

    This area of the Earth has been the deer's home far longer than it has belonged in any way to humans. Native Americans emigrated to this continent after the deer were settled, the Europeans arrived later still. All who have followed since have been here only a moment. If I feel that I accept Penelope into my world, she more greatly accepts me into hers. And maybe I'm wrong about inheritance. Her nine-million-year heritage on earth when compared to our own… but the words "our own" don't belong. At least today, I don't feel a "we" with humans too much, feel much more a "we" with the deer. I experience fleeting moments when people appear to be odd creatures. I watch and listen, see their mouths moving, hear the sounds, but can't always attach meaning. A hand offering food is unambiguous. It means "I care for you, I want you to be happy, to thrive, to be healthy." As the days pass, I feel a specific bond with this particular animal. I endeavor to live up to her trust and her expectations. When, in the course of her day, everything has been done well, I feel a rightness. I don't know how things will go tomorrow, but today Penelope has come, has found me, I have given her the best I have, which has been well received and seems to have been sufficient.

MARCH 3

I had a dinner date in the city last night. As Penelope has shown willingness to partially enter the house, for the first time I left her food inside the open door to the sunroom, on a table, confident that she would understand the arrangement. I also knew that none of the other deer would venture inside, that only Penelope had tested the safety of partially crossing the threshold and would enter with her head and front feet and take what was rightly hers.

Hours later, arriving home in the dark, I found that the bowl of chestnuts and soup had been nearly emptied, all the apple pieces, save three, were gone from their plate, everything had been taken neatly, nothing spilled. It was a new level of complicity between us, and a progressive solution to my brief absences, far better than disappointing her at sunset with a closed door and no one to greet her.

This morning she did not punish me by staying away, as she has often done. I may be projecting but I sense in her some private pleasure over what we had accomplished together the evening before, in my absence and her presence of mind. I had not only offered her food in a different way, I had communicated a new set of actions and she had correctly responded. She seemed this morning to be aware that she had known my intention and had shown me that she understood.

MARCH 4

After a particularly tender session of feeding and petting, Penelope has again gone into a series of spasms, lasting five or ten seconds, which involve seemingly involuntary muscle action, backwards scuttling, and a bucking of her head and neck, as if she were trying to expel something from her ears. As before, she has also extended her injured foot toward me. The last couple of times she entered this state I have simply stood with her, letting it happen without responding. Each time she has then begun with uncharacteristic force to lick my hands and arms. These licks are different from the ones which convey gratitude following a bowl of soup. The energetic licking carries an edge.

I wonder increasingly whether the edge is frustration. She is capable of asking for something and has a range of body language that lets me know what she wants. This specific sequence always includes extending her wounded foot. She must observe that she alone among the deer limps severely, the only one burdened with a broken limb and a misaligned body. Maybe her violent actions are a mute request to be healed, to be free from pain, to escape her injured body. Animals understand the healing process, licking their own wounds or licking the wounds of another that is injured, sometimes taking themselves away, lying in solitude, waiting for pain to ease or an injury to heal, rejoining their pack, herd, flock, or family once they recover.

Maybe Penelope has carried the expectation that her broken limb would mend. Perhaps her silent outpouring of combined motion says "I am telling you! I don't want to be this way anymore!" She has learned that I often understand her communication, that I can fulfill other of her desires. She knows by my committed presence and by my actions that I wish to give her what she needs and wants. I understand her request for another apple, know when she is asking me to take away her soup bowl—"I have had enough"—understand when she demands that I come to her. She has several times communicated to me that I have some scent on my hands which she finds objectionable—if I have perhaps touched the dog, that she won't eat until I have gone in and rewashed—and she has seen that I obey her request. She knows that I have understood when she feels afraid, and that I take steps to calm her fear. She knows that I have understood not only that she can't come onto the property at the moment, but also that I know why, and so have carried her food to her, waiting with her until her threatening mother has departed. She knows that I understand why she prefers the dog to be inside rather than out while she is eating, even though she knows the dog will not hurt her, that it is a preference but not a demand. And when, observing her anxiety, conveyed by repetitive squinting, I take the dog inside, her immediate relaxation, the cessation of squinting, shows that I have understood what she wanted. Her then moving toward me is a further acknowledgement that I have done as she wished.

Such interactions indicate that Penelope's thoughts are sometimes concrete and other times conceptual. They show that she relies on me to understand what she is thinking and that I will be able to act upon our communication. "I would prefer that the dog be inside" is fairly abstract. "I am in pain and I am tired of living this way" is abstract in a different sense, yet if I am able to understand and respond to the first, if I can address and correct her discomfort, why can I not also act upon the second request?

When, in her eyes, I must seem able to do so much, why don't I do the most important thing, to help her heal her broken foot and alleviate her pain? Given the loss of her relationship with her mother, I have been the responsive presence in her life. It seems natural that any desire should be directed at me.

If such is Penelope's thinking, it is somewhat accurate. I am not entirely unable to heal her or to take away her pain. I have certain extended powers, if not in my own hands then in the shared hands of others. Early in my connection with Penelope I spoke about her to my veterinarian, Dr. Lisa Schenkel. After an appointment where she had attended to Monkey, I said "May I ask you a deer-related question?" I described Penelope, a bit of her history and her condition, and asked whether there might be a way to mend her broken foot. I had a vivid fantasy of driving Penelope to the vet's office, watching as Dr. Schenkel held the foot gently in her hands, trying its range of motion, listening, palpating to find exactly where the problem was, and telling me how it might be addressed.

I imagined Penelope returning home, following surgery, on a tender but corrected foot, taking her first proper steps, with her legs, shoulders, and spine adjusting to their newly natural positions. I could see her learning to walk, then beginning to run, not from fear, as she has been forced to do, but running for joy, running for play, keeping pace with the other deer, leaping through and over the stream at dusk.

All of that might be possible, yet for any of it to occur, Penelope would need to be transported to the clinic. I would need to place a halter around her neck and lead her into the back of a vehicle, perhaps a horse trailer, which would almost certainly cause her great alarm and fear. She might reasonably feel at that moment that her trust had been manipulated and misplaced, that I had all along intended her harm and was now betraying her. To avoid that, she would need to be sedated, by placing a sedative in her food. Transported to the vet, she would then need to be kept still, in an enclosure, and x-rayed. If surgery were deemed advisable, she would be anesthetized, operated on to reset the foot and leg, sutured, bandaged, given splint or cast, and kept immobile while she healed. Then she could be transported home, perhaps again requiring sedation, and released into her proper environment. Weeks would have elapsed.

The success of an operation might be complete, partial, or minimal. Her musculature and skeleton would need to redevelop to accommodate a different leg configuration. Penelope's feelings at being taken from her environment and placed in an alien confinement, surrounded by strangers, fed whatever might be provided by the vets and by me, experiencing different kinds of pain than those she was used to, might be upsetting to her in ways and degrees I can't imagine. If I were able to visit each day, what role would she imagine I was playing in such massive disruption? With each visit she might expect me to bring her home and be upset when, time and again, I left her there. Would she tie the stress, dislocation, and pain to me, unable to comprehend that any of it was for her own good, not knowing whether she would ever again live at liberty under the sky and in the woods? She might feel confirmed that after every test she had placed between us, I had in the end fulfilled her worst fears and violated our pact that she would above all remain free. Once home, would she trust me again?

Dr. Schenkel said that without any veterinary intervention Penelope would adapt to her condition, that the best course was to continue as we were. She seems to have been right. Although Penelope exhibits varying levels of pain, she does quite well in her reduced state of mobility. She has acquired privileges the other deer do not have. Even as she will never be who she would have been had she not been injured, her life has changed for the better from what it was one year ago. By watching her sister, I can visualize Penelope's alternative life. While Daisy has had hardships, Penelope has a harder yet richer life, in part through her compensatory connection to me. She alone has my love, on which she visibly thrives. I believe that she is carrying a fawn and will soon have a true family.

MARCH 11

With record high temperatures the past week, one of the maple trees is in bud and I have heard the combined birdsong that heralds spring, ahead of schedule by several weeks. People who have been in semi-hibernation since November are once again walking in the late afternoons, lightly dressed, some conveying a mixture of pleasure and the concern that we are experiencing unambiguous signals of climate change. Penelope is visibly enjoying the warm days and nights. Standing together in the gentle air of predawn, sharing a state of silent grace, nothing else is needed.

I have made plans to soon be gone for two days. I hope that with food left for her, something Barbara and Frank have agreed to participate in, Penelope will know that I am still providing for her. Yesterday I tried an experiment, for the second time, to see if she would enter the house by a couple of feet to get her food without my being here. Late in the afternoon I set the small table just inside the open door of the sunroom and placed her chestnut bowl and a plate of cut-up apples on it. I went for a long walk, deliberately staying away longer than I might. Heading home, a few minutes from the house, I got a text from Barbara telling me that Penelope had been standing at the open door, looking at her dinner but not taking it. Barbara had kindly walked over and carried the table outside, where Penelope then ate. Barbara's next text told me that Penelope was still outside the house, and when I pulled up a few minutes later she was lying on the grass.

It was an unusually peaceful evening, silent and still, and it was remarkable in other ways. Even though she has always been wary in the presence of other people, even at a distance, Penelope had not run when Barbara came to the house but had accepted her assistance. Having eaten her chestnuts, her soup, and apples, Penelope then lay down and waited for me. This may indicate that she wants our loving contact as much as she wants the food. We stood in the diminishing light. In a few minutes, her family approached. Penelope stayed at my side. While mother and daughter eyed each for a long moment, I stared at Castle until she turned and walked away. The others stayed. Penelope was in the company of her sister and two half-siblings, all within a circle of seven or eight feet.

Although Castle would have been tolerated, she understood she was not welcome. She had not wanted Penelope. I did want her. My love was stronger than her rejection, stronger than the combined adversities of pain, weakness, cruelty, damage, and isolation. In the evening's stillness, Penelope's long-sought reunion with her family was happening. I tossed pieces of apple to the others while Penelope ate from my hand. The air was soft, the Earth seemed aware of early spring ascending. A very light rain began, the world at ease with itself and its creatures. Penelope and her siblings were having dinner together. It was one of the most peaceful moments of my life.

MARCH 21

I will need to be away for the next three days. I will leave large bags of cut apples in a cooler by the door and Barbara has agreed to put out Penelope's food twice each day. In my tenuous faith that Penelope might understand something different in my tone, I have tried to tell her that I won't be here. I have no choice and have planned the trip so that I will be away for the minimum time possible. I will not leave until after her dinner on Sunday, catching the redeye to L.A. My return flight is another redeye, scheduled to get into JFK around five o'clock Thursday morning. My car will be in short-term parking to speed the trip home and at that hour, with light traffic, I should be here for Penelope's breakfast, around six.

MARCH 26

While away, my thoughts were of Penelope and the three thousand miles between us. Anxious as to how she was faring. I was slightly distracted during tightly scheduled meetings with producers, director, cinematographer, casting agents, and others planning production of a feature from one of my screenplays. During table reads and working lunches on sunny poolside terraces, which should have been pleasurable, I was no doubt tapping my feet, focused on getting home. Everyone knew why.

Because my return flight had gotten in late, causing me to miss the morning with her as I had planned, Penelope and I had not seen each other for four days when she showed up the following dawn. I was extremely happy to see her.

She took a few warm chestnuts from my hand. Then she bit me. Hard. She has never bitten me before. She is always careful to avoid hurting me, especially with her strong molars, which can easily crack walnuts, and which today she brought down on my fingers. In case there might be any doubt as to her intention, any sense that the bite was an accident, she reared up on her hind legs and lunged toward me, going at me with both front feet. Nothing like it had ever occurred, and this is almost certainly her expression of anger at my absence, an escalation from her more passive protests of staying away and refusing food.

MARCH 29

After the week of disruptions caused by my having been gone four days, and three further days of her expressing her upset toward me, Penelope seems happy to have our reliable patterns of peaceful visitation and feeding. She is, if anything, more physically affectionate than before, rubbing her face against my torso over and over, more fully in possession of her place on the property, more aware of her unique entitlements. I am reminded of so many patterns of inter-human relations. When devotion has been thrown into question, its reconfirmation and the relief from uncertainty bring enhanced joy.

Time

There are those who assert that nonhuman animals live in the present and have no conception of elapsed time, but I find evidence to the contrary. For most dogs, the sight of a suitcase being taken from the closet and packed is not a neutral event but is emotionally charged. A dog who has lived for a while understands by this that very soon its owner will leave for a period of time—generally a dreadful prospect—or perhaps that the dog will accompany the master to a new or different location, often with joyous anticipation. The trip in the car, which soon follows, also implies uncertain futurity—"Am I going to the sitter's, a kennel, a friend's, where I will be left, or are we hitting a familiar highway which I know leads to Cape Cod and that place by the water where we've stayed, the beach I run on, the shop that lets me come in for muffins?" The dog will search for any sign to guide its expectation.

When the dog has been left for a period, the strength of feeling expressed at the sight and sound of the master's return is a reflection of time elapsed since the separation. A reunion after a few hours is milder than a reunion after a couple of days, which in turn is smaller than the near-hysterical wailing and dancing which accompany a reunion following a week apart. The dog is not living in a moment which simply happens to revolve around the sight of its master. The sighting is conditioned by elapsed time, which has been felt in a measurably cumulative sense. I may leave my dog to walk down the driveway and retrieve the mail, which takes two or three minutes. I may go to the post office, a trip of twenty minutes, may go into the city for four or five hours, may travel by air to a distant city and return a week later. During the long separation, the dog may be living with some anticipation of the reunion, imagining, looking forward to, perhaps visualizing a likely future event. She will see me appear from a certain direction, enter through a specific doorway. I will place her in the car. We will drive home, exit the car, walk toward the house, open the door. The dog literally runs to find her favorite stuffed animal. There follows a period of joyful reunion with the toy, lasting a few minutes, during which she reassures herself that it still belongs to her and has not been taken, changed, or moved. This is in marked contrast to her mild-to-nonexistent response at the sight of the stuffed animal after she has been away from it for several hours.

The changing light of an afternoon carries the likelihood of the daily walk, and when four o'clock arrives Monkey will signal that she wants me to stop working. The signs of four o'clock are very different in June than they are in December, yet she knows its arrival, sometimes to the minute, perhaps adjusting day by day. The ending of the walk carries the promise of dinner. These events are not confined to their moment. If they were, if the dog had no sense of elapsed time and its duration, the dog would be surprised continually by what was happening, would react equally to every event no matter its sequence or scheduling, as they do when forced to fluidly adapt to an unfamiliar, newly experienced string of events.

In relation to death, there may be a disruption in a nonhuman animal's sense of time. From the day Monkey came to live here, at two months old, she had never been without Una, a constant presence in her life. Una was nine years old when Monk arrived and she taught her about living in the house and on the property. Una respected the boundaries of the yard and never went outside them. She showed Monk how to do the same, and neither of them ever needed to be leashed. They slept, ate, walked, played, and traveled side by side. Monkey was sensitive and attentive to Una's well-being, to the point that she several times woke me in the night to alert me to some anomalous condition of Una's health. As Una approached death, Monk was beside her and sat with her as she died. Monk stayed with Una's body while I went to dig the grave.

When Una's grave was ready, I took the coat I had worn during our seventeen years together and wrapped her in it, with its sleeves encircling her, so that in death she would have my arms around her. I carried her outside. Monk followed. I lowered Una into her grave and settled her well. I got out and with the shovel began gently placing earth on top of her body, always the hard moment for me. Lowering the body into the grave feels of a piece with all the life which came before. The body is still a part of the living, above-ground world. Actions can still be reversed. The first shovelful carries finality, the deposit of earth marking the beginning of a permanently different state.

I may not have been the only one to sense this. As soon as the third shovelful was placed, Monkey jumped into Una's grave and began to dig her back up. She may have wondered why I was burying Una, who was not as she had been, but in Monk's eyes may have been only asleep. I reached down, lifted Monk, and placed her at the graveside where she could watch.

For months afterward, Monkey was visibly altered. She has a large heart and loves boldly. She had experienced losses of people who had entered her life and left it, but this was her first look at death, at least the death of a soul with whom she had shared her days and nights, shared her home, her food, breathed the same air, and now Una was gone. Monk had seen me participate in this transition, had seen me place Una in the ground and bury her, and I wondered what she was thinking, whether she thought I may simply not have wanted

> *The list of what unites living creatures is long, the list of what divides us is brief.*

Una anymore, whether I caused her death, whether she herself would be next. She may fear that I too will one day leave her. The sound of Una's name now causes her clear distress—she will begin to whimper—and I try never to say it aloud. I cannot know whether she wondered or still wonders whether Una could reappear. From my own magical thinking, I have kept Una's bed and her large stuffed bear. I am uncertain as to the nature of death, in ways that do not cause me fear and which may provide some comfort. In contemplating Una's death, I think of Monk's loss, not my own. Loss has been a continuous companion all my life, rather than an exception, and I try to focus on who and what has come. The past year has been enriched by the unanticipated, daily presence of Penelope, a cause for celebration, a reason to think about time.

Penelope comes in the first light of day, and at the last, transitional moments which have always felt poignant to me. They may be similar for Penelope, her sense of time subtle and mysterious, and she honors the light and darkness to a degree I admire. Decades ago, I loved the sight of deer grazing in the last rays of sunset. I still love to see them and love much more to be a participant, feel grateful that Penelope's rituals of passage involve me and that I honor them with her. As I have come to rely on her presence at the extremes of the day, she has come to rely on mine, knows that I will be awake, waiting and prepared for her at sunrise. She can be quite sure that as sunset approaches I will observe the ending of day with her, watching the fading light, in gratitude for all that we have been given.

APRIL 5

Wind-driven cold rain fell for hours yesterday, and through the day I wondered if Penelope had found shelter. In anticipation of seeing her I had been warming her soup and, as it was almost dark and the rain had stopped, she appeared at the door. She drank her soup and ate the warm chestnuts, and I could feel how chilled she must have been.

This morning was well below freezing, unusual for the first week of April, more so following temperatures in the eighties just four days ago. She came at six thirty and was again happy for her warm soup, yet she was also on alert, staring into the semi-darkness. As the light rose, I could see what was diverting her attention. Her family was asleep on the property.

The young ones ambled over first. I tossed each of them a couple of apple pieces, and then Penelope stiffened slightly; her mother was approaching. Soon the whole family—Castle, Daisy, Juno, and Windsor—were standing in a semi-circle while Penelope received her breakfast and the physical affection that goes with it. Castle may have figured out that if she shows no aggression toward Penelope, I will feed her as well as her offspring, and she stood passively with the others, everyone receiving apples. Penelope stayed after they had moved away, and I fed her more.

My hands had been splashed with soup and then licked vigorously and were literally freezing. Penelope knows that when I put my hands in my pockets and say "That's it," our feeding session is done, but she did not want to leave, and I would soon find out why. Her family had all gone toward the neighboring property. When Penelope was ready to walk away, I went with her. She eventually neared the edge of the property and I turned and went back inside but kept an eye on her. It had been a peaceful morning, all five standing close together, everyone being fed. Castle had stood near Penelope and had walked away without incident. But the mother had been pretending, biding her time, and was now watching and waiting, hiding within the low branches of a stand of dense spruce trees. As Penelope passed, Castle sprang out at her like a leopard ambushing a gazelle and chased her violently. Penelope ran and kept on running. The mother stopped, standing nonchalantly. I stormed toward her, as I would toward any bully, shouting. Castle knows that I am Penelope's ally and her protector. She understands the benefit of acting passively in my presence. But her hostility is awaiting its moment. As soon as Penelope was away from my protection, her mother had sprung. I wonder whether Penelope's status as the favored deer incites greater animosity, envy, bitterness, whether it serves to sustain and perhaps increase her mother's aggressive feelings. Castle tries to deceive me, pretending to be kind, or at least indifferent, to one of her offspring when I am watching. As in human relations, cruelty erupts, comparable to child abuse that is often hidden from social workers, from friends, from other family members. Despite chronic reports from social service agencies that everything in a home seems normal, children may ultimately be found bruised, battered, or killed, no one having seen anything untoward. I am observing similar layers of truth and deception, that what happens in human families behind closed doors also happens here, behind dense trees, within a family of wild deer.

APRIL 11

I am in the unusual situation of being invested in the protection of another life while being largely unable to protect that life. Penelope lives wild and free, and each time she leaves I must trust in her instincts and her good fortune to keep her from harm. Her range is finite and well known to me, yet the greatest portion of it is beyond my vision. I am never so deluded as to doubt that sources of harm are still present when she is out of my sight. It takes only one sunrise or sunset when she fails to appear and I imagine the worst.

Worry is one price of love, even when the loved one is capable and strong. In Penelope's case there is the primary factor of her disability. She would be the easiest target if a coyote were to come into the area. Incapable of using her front hooves as weapons, she is essentially defenseless. Yet six weeks from now she will be two years old, and she has survived against formidable odds. She seems unafraid to move about on her own. Having committed to watching over her, I have done it as fully as I can. Seeing her become anxious or afraid, I have quietly said to her, "I won't let anyone hurt you." I have at times failed her in this.

Telling people about the way Penelope bit me upon my return after a four-day absence, everyone has read it similarly, as signs both of her anger at my not being here, that our daily times together matter, and that I am important to her. I know of no other person who has entered into a complex relationship with a deer. The emotional aspect of our connection is mysterious. The evidence of her happiness at being fed and cared for, at our mutual grooming, of being acknowledged, is unmistakable. When we're apart, the thought of her makes me smile.

When I see Penelope moving toward me from the south, it carries the excitement and relief that we experience at the approach of a beloved person. I know it is a substantial distance to cover on a broken limb. She comes at a cost and I cannot properly imagine her pain. There is plenty for her to eat in the woods and fields, especially now, fresh spring grass and tender buds, a great improvement over the deadened vegetation of winter. She does not need to endure the stress and pain of walking on these spring mornings, yet she comes, and in her responses to my occasional absence I am further confirmed that it is not entirely hunger for food which drives her. I believe she wants my love. When I am not here to give it, she has a reaction that expresses itself very much the way a human does who expects to be loved and is dashed, and she lets me know. To understand, I try to place myself in her body, to imagine the moment when, having waited—possibly for hours—she concludes that I will not show up. She turns and walks away. At that moment of decision, what hope has transpired and been disappointed? It is an experience we have all shared; someone has let us down. It is a hard feeling, particularly when we are young and a parent or a friend has seemingly abandoned us. As it grows dark, and cold, and we have waited and waited some more, we resign ourselves—they are not coming. We know the posture of such retreat, head downcast, shoulders hunched, a silhouette of acceptance and sorrow, read clearly from a distance.

Penelope has lived through the sustained rejection of her earliest days and there is no forgiveness for abandonment. Her feelings are reanimated and, as with people, it may be that such occurrences become cumulative, that my absence is not a single event but carries the combined weight of her first year of life, with its unimaginably solitary hours, the days and months of isolation. When I am not where she expects me to be, when she wants food or love and does not receive it, she may turn and walk away with not only the disappointment of the moment, but the uncertainty as to whether she may ever see me again, whether her trust has been foolishly given, whether she has been reconsigned to a life bereft of love. For many of us, small incidents can trigger massive emotions.

I had been gone on Tuesday evening. Penelope did not appear Wednesday. But this morning, after an absence of a day and a half, she came, late. She stood at a distance. I approached and offered her the bowl of warm soup, which she refused to take. I offered several pieces of apple, which she touched with her lips, then turned away from. She took nothing from my hands. It should no longer surprise me that she punishes me for my lapses. Her pattern has been repeated enough that I must attribute her behavior to my failure to be here when she has expected me. She seems to understand that I have self-determination, and that if I let her down it is because I have made choices. Although I have observed periodic moments of fleeting connection between her and a few of the other deer, it seems that her relationship with me is unique. I am a substitute, if incomplete, for the mother who abandoned her, and there is no room for me to fail her, no latitude to let her down in any way. With about five weeks to go until the expected delivery of her fawn, she will soon no longer be so alone, and it would be healthy if she could accept my occasional absences as something other than rejection.

APRIL 26

During the past few weeks there has been evident solidification in Penelope's sense of belonging—with me, on the property, in the world. And I wonder how the new life inside her has affected this, wonder what she knows, whether beyond the added nutritional requirements she feels greater strain when walking. A doe preparing for birth displays changed behaviors and will sometimes take herself away from her usual places several days prior to delivery. Penelope has stayed closer to the house, sleeping in the large leaf pile at the southern edge of the property. It is an ideal nest, a soft mattress that takes the weight from her body and broken limb, with the advantage of offering a direct view of the back door.

MAY 3

Wanting Penelope to know that I was there for her when she woke, I stood outside yesterday at five, drinking coffee. She stayed in her leaf bed, looking at me but not yet ready to rise. As it began to get light, she stood, shook herself to shed any clinging leaves and took several steps toward me. There was no one about, human or cervine, as she ate, and when she was well fed, she slowly ambled off.

The day developed gently, temperatures in the fifties, warming later in the afternoon. At eight in the evening she appeared again, and I have never seen her so hungry. She devoured her apples and ate her soup with a passion, licking the bowl utterly clean. Then she had more apples, nuzzling against my torso to encourage me in feeding her. She must have been eating spring greenery all day, yet she was famished, her unborn fawn taking its nutrition from her body.

MAY 9

Her hunger is astonishing. Saturday morning Penelope had a handful of warm chestnuts, followed by a bowl of soup with about thirty chestnuts in it. Then a Honeycrisp apple. A Lady Alice. A Fuji. A Golden Delicious, a Red Delicious, a Macintosh. She then looked at me as if to ask what was for breakfast. I brought out another bowl of soup and she polished it clean. This morning she was outside at five forty-five. She ate a breakfast the size of the one just described, went to the leaf pile, lay down, and napped for an hour, then she appeared at the door and I fed her the same amount again.

Penelope has given birth

She is altered by the birth, weakened, vulnerable, yet prepared. Her life has entered its new phase.

MAY 17

She came to me just before dark, her feet stained damp, vulva swollen, her pink udder full. She was in a state of emotional tenderness and vulnerability that so often characterizes transitions.

It was a feeling different from any we had shared, gentle in each other's presence. A subdued joy was silently upon us in the dusk. I fed her in a quiet, newly complicit way. Sharing our oneness, she was with me, yet her attention was elsewhere, on her hidden newborn. From the direction of her focus I could sense where she had placed her private treasure. She understood that I knew what had occurred, she knew that I was her partner.

I am so proud of her.

MAY 18

I awoke at four, to be ready to provide for Penelope when she came, hoping to get a glimpse of her baby before first light, when she would hide it for the day. At five she was outside, by herself, the light already appearing through the trees. She has come to me twice since the delivery and again I fed her, paying attention to her face and body. She is altered by the birth, weakened, vulnerable, yet prepared. Her life has entered its new phase.

MAY 22

In strange confluence, this date, over many years, has often held an abundance of life in various forms—love, pain, change.

Early in the morning I drove through the rain to Philadelphia to attend the funeral of the mother of one of my oldest friends. Through my friend's eulogy I learned that her mother had willed her death by voluntary starvation, rather than fade away. Born in Poland, she had been taken from her home by the Nazis at age fourteen, put into forced labor, then sent to Auschwitz. She was assigned a job in the SS officers' kitchen, and to keep her two younger sisters alive she managed to smuggle out food, hidden in her clothing. The smuggling was a crime which, discovered, would have sent her to the gas chamber. Liberated at nineteen, she met her husband in a displaced persons camp, they came to America, led a life devoid of self-pity or complaint, spent decades doing for others, providing for the greater humanity, raised a family of significant accomplishment, offered kindness and love in every direction. The funeral service may have been filled for many with hard self-reflection, as it was for me.

I drove home, the sun came out, the light deepened toward sunset, Penelope appeared. As I carried her soup bowl to her, she was standing in her usual spot. I began to feed her when, at the same moment, we both turned our heads to see a fawn-colored animal dart swiftly across the lawn, heading in the direction from which Penelope had come. It was a red fox. She stared at the fox. Then she looked at the bowl in my hands. She had perhaps been dreaming all through the rainy day of her warm soup and began to tear through that bowl, eating triple-time. But in a few seconds, she stopped abruptly. She turned in the direction the fox had gone, and she flew. With inadequate legs and unseen wings she streaked toward the spot she had hidden her baby, moving incredibly fast. I ran with her, although she far outpaced me. Catching up, I found Penelope standing guard in front of an overgrown area where her fawn was undoubtedly hidden. I could not see the fox, but it was nearby.

Standing beside Penelope, I thought of how her own mother had menaced her and wished for her death. I thought of how, only five days ago, Penelope had no one to protect and was now filled with protectiveness toward a new life, all her own, filled with impossible strength. Together we were standing sentry as the light faded to the amber of the fox and of Penelope's hidden fawn.

The two aspects of the day, one death and one new life, carry connections: survival against odds, threat and defense, the protection of the innocent, risking life to prevent the starvation of another. Images were coming forward from the 1940s, and from the present: willful

starvation as a form of protection against the pain of a pitiful end, an effort to claim one's fate, images of a young girl who may have dreamed of a savior but had none, who year upon year had no promise of salvation. The morning's service had included a line valuable to me: "I shall fear no evil for Thou art with me." The twenty third psalm, among the most beautiful expressions of ennoblement and trust, had been included at the request of the deceased, and I wonder what it may have meant to her during dark years when the word "evil" was insufficient. Those who endure fear as an army, as a group, even as a pair, at least have each other. Those who are alone in the face of evil experience what may be the deepest level of despair. I thought of Penelope, protecting her fawn against a predator, after all she had gone through, and she was not alone. I stood with her to protect her baby and I thought "Fear no evil for I am with you." I stayed with her, standing sentry together in the dark for a long time.

Awake in the night, knowing that a predator was close, I rose at three, made fresh chestnut soup for Penelope, and waited. Before five, she was outside again. She ate her breakfast with the zest of a night's hunger, not in the haste of fear, at peace.

Penelope

JUNE 3

No longer the isolated fawn, Penelope is now a mother, needed and loved. In her eyes and in her face, she shows enhanced self-possession. She has been coming each day to be fed, and I have seen her in the middle distance, cleaning and nursing baby Carol. I can usually tell where she has hidden her as the direction of her distraction is easily gauged. She had only come alone, until this morning. I looked across at the neighboring property to see Penelope being followed by her fawn. I called to her to come. She hesitated, seemed to be considering it, then moved purposefully in my direction, with Carol close behind, bringing her to meet me.

JUNE 9

Yesterday was replete with sun, rain, wind, and a range of light and color, a long day as we approach the solstice, and Penelope and Carol came early. Having lived three weeks, Carol has gained strength and poise, and even a bit of independence. She shows curiosity about my relationship with her mother.

Arranging her day to be as close to me as she could, Penelope came to the door repeatedly. She is nursing and is constantly hungry and I fed her four complete meals. She had more than twenty large apples and three bowls of soup. Carol watched us, and then Penelope nursed her, the three of us inches apart, as a family, which I believe is how Penelope regards us. As she was eating, two other deer wandered by. She went over and quietly drew near them, as if whispering a warning to disperse. When they didn't, she lowered her head and put her ears back, a well-understood signal, telling them to move on, and they did.

At midday the sky darkened and it began to rain. Penelope and Carol stood together under the red maple, in the same spot where, last August, Penelope and I had also sheltered from rain, and she had groomed me for the first time.

I stood a few yards away and observed them. In an illuminating moment, Penelope urged Carol to move, nudging her, almost lifting her off the ground, then did something I had not seen for several months; she went into one of her uncontrolled paroxysms, legs scuttling and kicking out wildly, body twisting and bucking for a few seconds. When, in the earliest stages of our physical connection, she had done this in front of me, usually after I had fed her, I had not understood what I was seeing. I had tried to research her behavior and could find nothing. But seeing it again in the presence of her baby, I understood; when she moves in that way, she is excited and happy and wants to play. Penelope had been asking me to play with her. She had treated me as another deer.

She learned through my response that her playfulness would not be reciprocated, and she stopped trying. Had I known what it meant I would of course have played with her. I'm so sorry I didn't do it. Now she has a proper playmate, and nothing has been lost. Her impulses have not been damaged, not through her maternal abandonment, nor through my inability to understand what she was trying to teach me. Her mother would not play, I would not play, but at the signal, Carol understood. Penelope's grace told me that life and love are stronger than their opposites, that the abandoning mother did not take from her the simple beauty of wishing for a moment of joy in gentle summer rain. Penelope was playing with her own baby.

At sunset, after the rain, Penelope came back. We stood in the last light, bright and cool, igniting each auburn hair along her neck and back, illuminating her translucent ears. Longing for the light to fade and take away the burden of more beauty than I could bear, I fed her strawberries, black grapes, fed her extravagantly, as much as she wanted, for every reason. This was her triumph, to be celebrated. We had lived through pain, fear, and uncertainty, the risings in the dark, endured the winter and the cold, all of it leading us here, a June day of survival, and I silently thought, "this is your prize, your literal moment in the sun. We have every richness, and it is all for you."

As it became almost dark, I urged her to go to Carol, who was resting nearby, invisible. At Penelope's approach Carol stood and they connected and nursed again while I watched.

The fullness of the day was not over.

At two thirty in the morning, Monkey began to howl in her sleep. I have heard her do so only two or three times in her life, a perfect coyote howl, somewhat muted while she slept, a howl which connects her with many thousands of years past, and I wondered what she might be dreaming. It took a second to realize that I had already been awake before she howled, she had not awakened me. I listened. Fully asleep, she was answering the call of a real coyote, somewhere outside, which we had both dimly heard. Soon I heard another sound, the bleating of a fawn, like the cry of a lamb separated from its mother. Fawns are not awake at three, they sleep through the night, and it was all wrong. I heard trampling hooves, then silence, enough to tell me that there was no need for me to rise and go out to protect the vulnerable. What had happened was done.

I did not sleep. I got out of bed in the dark with a sense of the inevitability of time, to begin the day, whatever it would hold. I waited. There was no one.

At first light, as Penelope and Carol came through the trees, they were more perfect in my eyes than ever. It was a joyful morning, yet something had happened, a fawn had been killed in the night. I believe I know who it was—a story for another time, with its own levels and layers. It is less painful than what I had most apprehended, as if one death is preferable to another, which in sad truth we must acknowledge it is, when we love.

It is now dark again, and I do not forget that this is another night, that last night's darkness was not the last of dark nights, that there may again be howling and sleep-howling in reply, bleating and running, silence and waiting. I should not forget that this is the price of attachment, and these the rules of engagement.

Penelope

JUNE 15

It has been four weeks and one day since Carol's birth. I laugh. I am like a new mother, reciting the exact age of her baby, but the universal parental precision is a reflection of how the world changes at the moment of delivery.

Around noon I found Penelope resting under her red maple. I joined her, standing beneath its branches, and fed her. Then I rested in the hammock, a few feet from her. As she lay down to resume her nap, she continually produced the vocal sound she never possessed before the birth of her fawn, but which is now a beacon to signal her own whereabouts. After twenty minutes, she rose and purposefully made her way to the edge of the property where she was swiftly joined by Carol, who had been resting in greenery.

An afternoon in June, sunny and dry. The shade of a red maple. Fresh apples, cut into bite-sized pieces, fed to her, a voice telling her how beautiful she is, what a good mother, how lovely is her baby. To nap in the shade under a protective gaze. To rise and join her fawn. To feel whatever pleasures she takes in nursing and grooming Carol, in being groomed by her in return. All of this follows a hard beginning, two years of pain, isolation, aggressive abandonment from her own mother. Yet I believe the most important change is an end to her solitude. Since Carol's birth she is different toward me and expresses a deeper level of closeness and trust between us. Carol looks to be entirely healthy and is being properly cared for by her mother. By nature's schedule she has entered the world during the most welcoming and gentle days of the year, everything in abundance.

JUNE 16

Since the night of the coyote, the night of crying and howling, Daisy's fawn has not been seen. Daisy is swollen as if lactating, and while it is hard to imagine, she seems to have lost another fawn, her second in nine months. Each deer has a life, an identity, and perhaps a destiny, and loss seems to be Daisy's. Yesterday, Daisy stood near Penelope while she was being fed. I threw many pieces to Daisy, a small gesture which I hope brought her comfort.

At four this morning, Penelope was waiting. I think she may have seen the lights come on in the house. I fed her chestnut soup, and we played the game we have been working on, where she eats some apple pieces from my fingers and some from the small wooden table. She has learned how to pick them up, with her lips and tongue, has indeed become quite good at getting them. I cut the piece. I place it deliberately on the table. She picks it up with one sure move. And we repeat. She clearly enjoys her new skill, a variation on being fed. She regards the little table as hers and claims it by rubbing her head and face against the under-edge. She had six large apples, licked the table for any residue, and asked for more, coming ever closer. I went in and got another two. She must be as hungry from nursing as she was from carrying her fawn in utero. After the apples, we walked off together in the direction of Carol, who was still asleep, Penelope picking up fresh maple leaves from the ground. To show that I understand their value, I occasionally picked up a leaf and fed it to her. At seven o'clock, as it was getting light, she was back at the door, this time with Carol, hungry again.

Carol is showing some independence and will wander away. Penelope often chooses to stay with me. When she comes to me by herself, it feels as if she is telling me that, although she enjoys having her fawn, it can be tiring and stressful. She seems to want some time where she is the one who is cared for. The need to keep her baby hidden will soon end and they will be a pair throughout the day and night.

If I had granted the film producers use of this property, nothing could ever have compensated for the damage done. My failure would have haunted me. As it is, the rewards of this moment are countless. The days are at their longest, the morning and evening light filled with amber. Carol is more than a month old. She is with Penelope much of the day and their oneness is evident, nursing, grooming each other, playing. When Penelope was alone and in pain, her life tenuous, I might have said to her, "There will be a day of warmth and sunshine, right where we are standing. You will have your own baby. You will care for her and she will love you. You will be healthy, and your pain will be less. This will be your home, and no one will try to chase you away. I will be here. The hard times will be gone."

JUNE 20

In the warm light, Penelope swept her head across my torso, licked my hands and forearms. She offered her broken foot, gently lunged at me, butted me with her head, gestures of intimacy, playing with me the way she plays with her fawn. I stroked the top of her head and her ears. I touched her twisted, folded leg.

Penelope

JUNE 22

At four thirty this morning, it felt as if Penelope, Carol, and I alone inhabited the world, until, midway through her soup, Penelope straightened, turned, and snapped to full attention. She was staring at a precise spot in the distance, her body tensed, ears erect. I could see only dense trees and other growth. Penelope did not move. In a moment, at two hundred yards, there appeared the fox.

One month ago, to the day, we had stood guard together to protect hidden Carol, who was then five days old, against this same red fox or another like it. This time, the fawn was with us, strong and healthy. The fox moved across our field of vision in its arrow-straight path and disappeared. Another half minute passed before Penelope relaxed and returned to her soup. As we progressed through the second and third courses of breakfast—apples, strawberries, grapes, more apples, and more berries—I pondered Penelope's senses. She could not at that moment have seen the fox, yet realized it was near. I question whether any sound could have been distinct enough to tell her its source. If her sense of smell told her a fox was nearby, she must have catalogued the scent of fox and filed it under "threat." It must be a precise scent, distinct from the various mammals living in her range, including dogs, squirrels, raccoons, skunks, possums, woodchucks, cats, other deer, and humans. Prior to the birth of her fawn, I had been with Penelope several times when we saw a fox and there was no such reaction. She knows that a fox is now a threat to her young fawn but was not, and is not, a threat to her, complex instinctive calculations. Penelope is two years old. Carol is her first fawn. In concert with giving birth, she received, or released, an updated range of reactions to her environment in the service of nurturing and protecting the new life.

I endeavor to live up to her trust and her expectations.

The Coyote in daylight

One morning, as Penelope was eating from my hands, I saw the coyote, thirty yards away, standing stock still, staring at her and at Carol, as prey. Penelope froze. I held my hands palm outward to her and said "It's okay, I've got this. You stay right where you are."

I went for that coyote, moving toward it straight and fast, with iron commitment to kill it bare-handed if need be, shouting "Get out! Out! Out! You go!"

The coyote turned and ran from me.

I walked back to the spot where Penelope and Carol stood, motionless. As I came close to Penelope her terror eased, her paralysis released, her back legs collapsed, and she spontaneously urinated over herself. She knew the coyote was not a dog, knew it was a predator more dangerous than a fox, capable of harming her and her fawn. She also knew that I am part of her world, and that I am her protector.

Last evening, Penelope and Monkey had their dinner together on the lawn, a few feet apart. It seems that since becoming a mother Penelope now recognizes Monkey as belonging to me in a way similar to the way Carol belongs to her, that she understands Monk's place in my life and that, even as Monk is related to wolves, coyotes, and foxes, she is no threat. Monk also seems to feel Penelope's easy acceptance and wants to be included in our connection, seems to enjoy watching me feed the doe.

The birth of her fawn brought Penelope to a new phase, and she is changed in ways I would never have thought myself capable of observing in a wild animal. She seems to enjoy being her new self. I increasingly experience her life as subtle and complex, and if the complexity is true of her, it must be true of all other creatures, ours for the knowing if we only look and listen.

Detachment and attachment

JUNE 26

Penelope lives uneasily in the world of deer and is not entirely one of them. They stand and watch as she and I touch each other. I can't know whether they think she is crazy, or whether they might envy her, but none of the deer in this vicinity have relationships with a human. The others often hover at the edges in hope of receiving some fragments of what I give her in abundance.

The deer seem to know that Penelope holds a place in a privileged space. Other people know that I hold a place in the same privileged space, literal and emotional, that Penelope and I have created together. The mutual detachment has allowed us to form our own floating world, the world of each other, hovering between human and deer habitations, in and amongst the same trees, grass, and water, feeling the same wind, the same rain and sun, yet differently.

Detachment allows for the exceptional. Throughout human history, detachment in an array of forms has been sought as a means of seeing, knowing, experiencing that which is otherwise inaccessible.

Detachment is a theme in religious tracts and in cartoons—the isolated holy man meditating on a mountaintop, sitting alone in a cave, seeking clarity, the thousand-mile journey by foot, always alone—for companionship is attachment and attachment obstructs the freedom needed for arrival at another plane. Through the portals of dreams, madness, solitude, music, drugs, fasting, alcohol, meditation, people have sought detachment in order to journey elsewhere.

Penelope's isolation was not sought but was forced upon her from her very earliest days, and she learned to survive alone. A deer fully attached to its environment and biological life may neither need nor desire a connection with a human. Although Penelope does not need me as she did, she wants our bond, and it is she, as much as I, who is eradicating the borders between us. She is sharing with me the thing I most deeply believe in, an act of transcendence, larger than that of race, language, culture, telling me she understands that connection exists soul to soul, the desire to erase boundaries existing here in a wild creature.

JUNE 28

Carol is six weeks old today. Every morning she watches from two feet or closer as her mother is fed and touched by me. Carol is startled by other humans when she sees and hears them. She has learned from her mother that I am trustworthy and she shows no fear of me. I wonder whether she has made a connection between Penelope's disability and our special bond and am curious as to whether she will follow her mother and begin to eat from my hand. Carol is healthy and is in alignment with her nature. If her exemplary life continues as it is, her mother's example may not carry meaning for her.

JUNE 29

Upon giving birth, Penelope began making a highly-specific vocal sound, intended to call to the baby when there is any separation.

As it is produced, her larynx can be seen to move up and down. The sound is akin to the rattle of a guiro, the Latin rhythmic instrument of a stick drawn across a serrated, hollow gourd. This morning when I heard the sound I was indoors. I assumed Penelope was calling to Carol, but when I went out, I saw the two of them standing side by side next to the house. Penelope was not calling to Carol. She was calling to me through the open window.

Her call suggests that she trusts I will recognize her voice and will respond. This is the essence of communication. When she calls to Carol she does so with those assumptions, and if she makes sound to get my attention it almost certainly carries the same expectation. I am not sensitive enough to note whether the call is exactly the same or whether it is a variation, distinctly different to her, as if she has names for each of us. Penelope is of a generally silent species and yet is sensitive to my vocalization and responds consistently to words and phrases I use in speaking to her. Today, she was speaking to me.

JUNE 30

Mid-afternoon yesterday, I heard a faint tapping. Sophia, a thoughtful and well-mannered eight-year-old neighbor, was at the door, her whole body turned inward, somber and hesitant, looking at me from a downcast face. "What's wrong?" I asked. "Is everything okay?"

Almost inaudibly, she whispered, "One of your baby deers got killed."

She had walked across the lawn by herself, to find me, while her mother, Mary, waited on the driveway. Sophia and I walked together and sighted down the driveway toward the road. A fawn lay on the pavement. I said to Sophia, "Thank you for telling me, sweetheart. I'm so sorry you had to see this."

I walked down the driveway. I bent and touched the body, which was still warm, but not breathing. The fawn had been killed minutes earlier, the blood which was pouring from its mouth a shockingly bright red, the freshest cadmium, so brilliant in the sunlight that it did not seem to be part of nature. I lifted the fawn from the road, and carried it up the driveway, where Sophia stood watching with Mary. At the far end of the driveway Sophia's older sister, Sarah, was openly crying, standing in the arms of her father.

What happened next is strange.

Sophia had said "One of your baby deers," and I know she regards me as the "deer man" and that by virtue of my connections with them all the deer are mine. I had, from that instant, told myself that the dead fawn was not Carol, because my fear of Carol dying was too great to allow it. I had held the dead fawn, carried it up from the road, and now, in a pivot from my earlier denial, I convinced myself of the worst possible scenario, that the fawn was in fact Penelope's baby. Carol's pattern of spots and her white foot markings essentially matched those of this fawn.

The fawn lay on the grass. I had promised Sophia I would give it a proper burial and I selected a place. Although the fawn was so small, its long legs necessitated a large hole. I dug a plot four feet long by three wide, three feet deep. It took me two and a half hours—there were many rocks in the earth—and as I dug, I replayed the morning. While I had fed Penelope, I had said to her, "Look what you have. It is a perfect June morning. You have your baby, who is so good, healthy, and strong, truly the most beautiful fawn in this whole neighborhood. You have strawberries and grapes and Honeycrisp apples. You have chestnut soup. You are healthier than you have ever been. This is your home, and everyone knows it is yours. Anyone who was mean to you has gone away. Look at the love we have, all the love, so much love there isn't any left in the world, it is all right here."

The fragility of life seemed to fill the fresh void. I thought about all that had gone into Carol's new life—Penelope's unlikely survival, her pregnancy and seven-month gestation, the carefully chosen food. Six weeks and one day was as long as the fawn got to live in the world, but it had been a fine six weeks, the most beautiful time of year. Two hundred and one days of gestation, and forty-three days of life.

I thought of Penelope's hunger in the morning, more than simple need for food but also for the sharing and giving, the touching, which she did not want to stop. "Hold nothing back," I thought, as I dug the small grave. "Give what you have and give some more because we don't know if it will be our last chance before life suddenly turns and that which we love may be gone."

I laid the fawn gently in the grave, placed a blanket of fresh green leaves over the fawn's face, and began to cover the body with earth. I filled the grave, smoothed the earth, and placed a ring of stones around the perimeter. It was five thirty and I expected Penelope to appear in half an hour. I did not know what I might read in her eyes and in her motions and I needed good things for her. I quickly took a shower and drove to the store where I bought strawberries and the best apples. When I pulled into the driveway at home, I saw Penelope waiting. A few yards behind her stood Carol.

Carol had not been killed, yet another fawn had, a new life ended on the road. A new mother would be searching for her fawn, a mother who had undergone seven months of gestation for six weeks of life. It was no less a miracle, no less a bond broken, no less a loss. I had been engaging my fear, forcing myself through the process as an inoculation against the event that Carol might not survive. I don't know what part of me might have known I was burying another fawn.

I am wrong to be relieved that it is not Carol, and yet I am relieved. Penelope still has her baby. It is nature, the nature of family, human nature, the selective and selfish nature of love, that we value one life above another, mourn one death beyond another, when all the living and the dead are equally alive and equally dead. Survival is only the momentary avoidance of death, a threat which renews itself constantly for us all.

At sunset the mother of the dead fawn stood on the road, sniffing the path where her baby had last lived, and where it had died. The mother is Clover, a contemporary of Penelope's, who has been generally aggressive toward her. The aggression stopped when each of them had a fawn. I had been stern with Clover in defending Penelope, but I now felt compassion for her. It is the third time I have watched a doe search for a fawn who is no longer alive.

It had been an intense day, for the young life which ended, for the bereft mother, for Sophia witnessing death, and for me, digging yet another grave.

My failure to protect the vulnerable continued this morning. As I was feeding Penelope, Carol nearby, Clover ambled over, newly alone. I tossed a few pieces of apple to her. When feeding was done, she and Penelope strolled together, eating vegetation, then Clover suddenly chased Penelope and she ran. It is said that in humans, anger is redirected pain, and so it may be in deer.

JULY 1

Much that can happen to the living is happening in the world of the deer.

Late in the morning an unusually pale blonde fawn appeared. She is the same age as Carol and seems to be orphaned. She lay down in one of the leaf beds. An hour later, as Penelope and Carol arrived, the fawn approached Penelope. It is understood that deer will not adopt, even lactating mothers who have lost their own will not nurse an orphan, but Penelope nuzzled the fawn, face to face. Carol then did the same. Penelope treated the fawn with tenderness and groomed her as if she were her own. When finally they moved toward the next property, the orphan followed them. She is probably too young to survive without her mother's milk and may try to nurse from Penelope. For her rare coloring I have named her Ashley.

JULY 2

Before sunrise, Penelope came, followed by Carol and by orphaned Ashley. As the two young ones browsed, I fed Penelope warm soup, strawberries, grapes, apples. And as I was feeding her, there appeared a buck with velvet-covered antlers, only my second sighting of an adult male since last fall's breeding season. He came onto the property and stood watching Penelope as she ate. Carol went to him and they sniffed one another. I wondered if he was her sire, here to check on his family. I wanted him to stay and tossed a few pieces of apple in his direction. Then came Castle, whom I had not seen in many weeks, with her own new twin fawns, and they too each greeted the buck. He may be the father of many of the fawns in the area.

Each day, Carol is larger, stronger, and less vulnerable. I want her to become an adult, to stand with her mother and act as an ally, to defend her. I would like to see Penelope surrounded by her own family so that she cannot be singled out for bullying. Penelope's mother, having judged her unworthy of life, had it wrong. Penelope has survived cruelty not visited upon any of the others, has endured unique challenges and has earned her place. She has shown herself the one most fit for survival, with the strongest will, possessed of the largest spirit.

"The last shall be first" is suggested in the Bible. This "last" has become what, in our initial hours of contact, I told her she was, the best one of all the deer, the most beautiful. I told her she was not alone, and she is not alone. I told her I was watching over her, and I watch over her. I told her that if she came to me, I would care for her, and she has come, and I care for her.

JULY 5

The longer I watch the deer, the easier it is to see that each has an individual temperament, and a distinct level of dominance and submission. It seems equally clear that there may be no hard and fast biological or evolutionary imperatives that determine the nurturing of offspring. In light of her own abandonment, Penelope's tenderness toward her fawn raises questions. The notion that love can be given when it has not been received is supported here. And while we may say that maternal love is simply instinct, it was not Castle's instinct to care for Penelope after her injury. I cannot visualize Penelope abandoning Carol should an injury impede her movement. It might be that Penelope's own condition alters her position relative to her fawn's viability and health, that she might have a sense of empathy or oneness should her own fawn be less than perfect.

  I have watched Castle chase Penelope, as well as others, in a menacing way and keep on chasing her when she runs. I have charged at her to protect Penelope. I have stood in front of Castle, eye to eye, and faced her down, and on the bitterly cold evening of Anthony's death I carefully observed Castle as she searched for her son. She stood on a high point and scanned the woods across the road, stood for hours, watching for any sign of him as it grew dark. In darkness she sniffed the hollow in the snow where Anthony had slept the previous night. From his birth she had rarely been more than a few feet away from him. She, Anthony, and Daisy had slept in a tight circle every night, had come together to the door several times a day through the winter, each in their specific spots, being fed in reliable sequence. Unable for the first time to see or find her son, Castle came later that night and stood looking at me in a way she hadn't done before. I felt compassion toward her, I looked into her eyes, I wanted to be able to explain, because I knew what she did not, knew that her son was gone and would not come back. I had stood beside Anthony while he lay dying on the road. I had called for help. I had no way to tell Castle that he had been shot through the head by a police officer, that it took two blasts of the shotgun to end his suffering, knew that Anthony's body had been picked up from the road, and loaded onto a truck, and driven away.

  In recent weeks, within feet of the house, two young fawns have been killed. I buried one of them last Wednesday, the other was taken by a coyote the night of Monk's howling. The bereft mothers are Clover and Daisy. It is simple to imagine that orphaned Ashley would be accepted by Daisy or by Clover, both of them lactating and absent their fawns, yet neither has taken her in. The one who has accepted her is Penelope. Last night and again this morning Ashley has been with Penelope and Carol, seemingly a third member of their family. The information I have been able to find suggests that a fawn can survive without nursing from its mother after the age of two months. Ashley is far younger. Penelope survived without her mother's milk at a very early age. She has been physically tender with the orphan, grooming her, and it feels like a small step from there to nursing. Ashley looks to be healthy, if fragile. She lies in one of the leaf nests, waiting, and when Penelope and Carol come, she rises and joins them.

Contrasting Castle's devotion to her healthy, deceased offspring with her animosity toward her disabled fawn, one was mourned, the other repeatedly rejected. Penelope knew who her family were, knew they were living on this property, tried to rejoin them, to come home, and each time she was driven away. If Castle had been able to speak, she might have told Penelope, "The sight of you revolts me." As harsh as this appears, the words parallel the actions. I may be preconditioned to interpret my observations of Castle's behavior. I may be projecting some of it. I also may be more clear-eyed than I allow, may temper some observations and interpretations from an excess of caution about anthropomorphizing. There are many unambiguous signs that Penelope loves Carol and regards her as a partner. She is constantly aware of Carol's location, always keeps an eye on her, unconsciously orients her body toward Carol, even when they are separated by hundreds of feet and visual contact is obstructed.

I am unsure about Clover, whose fawn was killed one week ago, and her own temperamental impulses. Judging from her behavior, Clover has a hard inner core, akin to arrogance or self-centeredness. Her level of animus toward Penelope does not carry a biological or evolutionary imperative. Penelope is not Clover's offspring. She takes nothing from her. They are not competing for males, who mate with many females during the season. There is sufficient space and food for everyone. It seems to be only meanness that drives Clover's aggression, and in terms of cruelty toward Penelope she takes second place, after Castle.

JULY 8

I try to be scrupulous when drawing conclusions about the deer from my observations, and to ask whether any assessment may be projection. Projection is a large component of personal interaction, an expression of our entrapment within our own point of view; because we individually experience an emotion or have a response in a given situation, we assume others must feel or perceive the same thing we do. How often are we told "you must be disappointed", "you must feel thrilled"? Folded into the word "must" is the overtone of command.

It may be rare for us to listen to and understand what another person feels, sees, hears, believes, and to accept that it is possibly, if not probably, different from our own responses and perceptions. Reflexive projection is an impediment, difficult to overcome. It is an extension of the same confinement to insist that no one else could feel what we feel. In either case we place ourselves in a central position of arbitration and declare definitively that we can determine the feelings, perceptions, and beliefs of another. The core and essence of love may lie in being able to set aside our own feelings and responses in order to be allowed to know and to internalize the feelings of another. This, by definition, is empathy.

There is a historic system of belief that another group does not feel what we feel, that our use of "we" does not embrace "them." America's slave owners espoused the position that slaves did not feel pain. It was propagandized during the Second World War that the Japanese were a substantially different species of human. There are those who insist that animals do not feel pain. "We" may feel pain, hunger, fear, but that is "us." "They" are different. To address systems of comparison or contrast demands diligence. The emotions of a domesticated animal may appear to be similar to, or different from, human emotions, but it is apparent to most who live with a dog or cat that these animals have emotions. There are those who argue that what appears to be emotion is some other thing—instinct, reflex—but such an argument usually rests less upon observation than it does on a preconditional belief in human exceptionalism.

The list of what unites living creatures is long, the list of what divides us is brief. The more time I spend with Penelope the more I marvel at what we share. Biologically, our structural and organic components are essentially identical. Skull, jaw, teeth, spinal column, vertebrae, limb bones, ribs, muscles, tendons, joints, ears, eyes, nostrils and olfactory organs, tongue, lungs, digestive system, a beating heart, arteries, veins, capillaries, nerves, skin, and hair. Her brain and mine each process actions, learned, adaptive, and reflexive responses, and memory.

Some of her senses are capable of greater reception and discernment than my own. As her sense of smell is vastly superior to mine, so might be her sense of taste. An herbivore, she may catalogue limitless varieties of flavor and fragrance. I have observed her eating at extremely close range, daily, for over a year. She has highly tangible preferences for certain fruits, and varieties of those, very clearly loves red grapes over green, a fully ripe strawberry over one less or overly so, a Kiku or Smitten apple over a Sonya, a Golden Delicious over a Red, a Honeycrisp above all, a Granny Smith never.

> *"Your mother missed out on a good thing. She didn't know what she had."*

She clearly enjoys warm soup over tepid, chilled berries over those room temperature. She recoiled one morning from soup that was too hot and would not approach that specific ceramic bowl again. I still feel terrible for having caused her pain and probably always will, and I replaced her soup bowl with one which looked very different, which she accepted. Another morning, when her chestnuts had sat too long on the stove, repeatedly re-heated, she turned away from them. She wants her breakfast in specific sequence, and if in winter I try to give her grapes before soup she will politely refuse by turning her head aside. And someone who might say that she is a wild animal who eats what she can find would be correct. A human forced to live outdoors and eat only available wild nutrients would also take what they could get. It would neither negate nor have bearing upon the human's ability to tell good food from bad. Deer who scrounge in the February slush and snow for dead leaves and spruce needles have little way to convey that those do not make an optimal dinner. They have no autonomous means of getting fresh New Zealand apples or California strawberries. Provided with good fruit and warm soup, the deer will display a passionate preference and appreciation.

JULY 12

I offered Penelope blueberries for the first time. She pressed her face into my torso and swept my right arm down, her signal for "more please." I gave her a handful, followed by sliced strawberries, red grapes, green grapes, more berries.

JULY 18

Since the birth of Carol, my twice-daily times with Penelope have been constant. On Saturday evening I was in Manhattan, unavoidably, the first evening in a while I had missed being there for Penelope's feeding. I arrived home well after midnight, set the alarm for four fifteen, and when I awoke I had only had three hours sleep. I

Penelope

did not care and wanted to be there for Penelope and Carol when they arrived. I sat outside and waited. They did not come. My first absence of an evening in over two months was followed by her first absence of a morning in that time. I feel confirmed that she punishes me in kind, for letting her down, for not living up to her expectations, possibly rekindling her feelings of abandonment. The sequencing is precise and reliable and has its effect upon me. Apart from missing the joy of contact, I know by now that her absence, her standing me up for our regular date, carries intention and is meant to tell me that I have hurt her, and is meant to hurt me in return.

Having not seen her, my day was unsettled. It was near dusk when she finally appeared. She held back, standing at the edge of the property, looking at me. I went to her and motioned for her to come. I offered a strawberry. She touched it, took it between her lips, spat it on the ground, and walked away.

If this pattern of behavior over three days, and its distinction from the pattern established over the previous months, does not reflect Penelope's emotional life, I have no other way to explain it. It is an abbreviated form of what we went through last fall when I was absent for several days. She has invested her trust in me, and when I honor that trust without fail, we share reliable happiness. When I violate it and am unable to explain why, or that it is temporary, her response mirrors common human response in similar situations. From her perspective, I may exist to care for her. At the moment she is not far wrong, and while there are things she may not understand, perhaps there are things I do not understand. I may not fully realize how much our time means to her, may not understand the investment she made in trusting me and allowing me to touch her. I may not know the full weight she carries from being rejected by her mother.

She does not strictly need the food I give her, particularly now in summer when there is plenty for her to eat. But in transposed form, all that we share may be that which was denied her at a time when fawns receive the love of their mothers and siblings, a time when Penelope was alone, unfed, untouched. A single evening when

I am not here may tear open a wound, in the way an adult who was abused as a child will forever react to any hint of abuse from a partner. She has reliably shown her responses to my temporary absence. She withdraws.

This morning, I arose at four fifteen and waited. Penelope approached me directly. She enthusiastically ate chestnut soup, strawberries, grapes, blueberries, raspberries, and apples. When she was finished, she licked me and groomed me. Then she went to Carol, nursed her and groomed her in the same way. We are back on track.

JULY 20

Today's Times carries an article on a government proposal to reintroduce cougars into the northeastern states as a means of controlling the whitetail deer. Willing the death of a deer by cougar attack is as appalling to me as willing it on a person, imagining the terror, the pain, the sustained rending of flesh, the victim's bloody struggle to live. A deer that has been killed leaves behind family. I have witnessed the grief among them.

The fragility of life and volatile certainty of death are brightly underscored by my knowledge of Penelope. She has paid her dues, paid up front, in full. She has suffered, has proven her courage and her strength. Her fawn has so far led a charmed life of a few weeks, and I do not want Carol ever to suffer.

To invest emotionally in another life, when that life is human, allows for a degree of cooperation from the loved one in their safety and survival. We can instruct a child in navigating the world. We can provide a degree of shelter for children and adults. We can ask for the end-of-journey phone call to let us know they have arrived safely. I am mostly helpless when it comes to guiding Penelope's days and nights, apart from the morning and evening visits, which are at her discretion and under her control. If she approaches or leaves by crossing the road, I cannot do much to change it. I know because I have tried. If there should appear a coyote in the night, I am not there in the woods to drive it away. The moments where I have been able to provide some protection allow me to feel vigilant. I have physically protected Penelope from aggression and know that she observed and understood the defense she received, as on the morning of the coyote and the evening in May when we stood side by side to guard five-day-old Carol against the red fox. I can demonstrate my protective intentions, can show Penelope that she is safe with me and that she is loved. I can encourage her to live here and not wander past this zone of relative safety, but I cannot guarantee or enforce anything.

I do not know the chances of Penelope living out her full life, or Carol's chances of reaching adulthood. The road claims deer, has done so right in front of me. There are orphaned fawns and fawnless mothers now. Penelope's brother was killed, Daisy's fawn was killed, as was Clover's fawn, whom I picked up from the pavement and gently buried. A nameless mother of triplets was killed three years ago, right here. I heard the collision, heard the euthanizing shotgun blast from the merciful cop, who came when I asked, heard another collision and another merciful shotgun blast which took Penelope's brother Anthony minutes after he and I had been standing in the winter sun with a basketful of apples.

In the face of my love for a wild animal, I am aware that she is a continuation of the deer who lived on this spot of earth in earlier centuries, that she is on a continuum of life which has been successful, which has survived unchanged through human habitation of what has been cervine habitat for thousands of years. She and I now live in our moment. We may also live in a broader aspect of time, its flux and flow, the ways it folds, which is invisible and inapprehensible, at least yet. I know so little about any of it.

I know less about living souls, less about the nature of time, than I do about the chair I am sitting in. The chair too is moving through time, is a survivor, made in the late 1700s from trees which had grown a century or longer. Made of living matter transformed, it has outlasted any mammal associated with it, and can continue to do so indefinitely. As it was being made there may have been deer close by, smelling the fresh-cut wood, perhaps listening to the chairmaker singing to himself. In 1780 there were no cars to harm the deer. They gave birth to fawns in the exact manner that Penelope gave birth to Carol, they nursed and groomed and called to each other as they do today. Maybe the craftsman found beauty in them and found peace in their presence, as do I.

It all goes. What seems most durable and most evanescent is love, immune to the sweep of time and the changes in the world, for in the moment it is felt, when love is expressed, it is fully alive.

AUGUST 8

Observing Penelope at close range, it would require willful blindness to deny that she feels emotions toward her fawn, and that the fawn feels emotions toward her, to ascribe to every instance of expression an instinctual motive and character. The basic interactions between deer would look different if they were only functional steps toward survival.

To watch a mother and her young fawn greet each other, to see the way they call to and look for the other, the after-nursing grooming and touching, forces me to contemplate the withdrawal from a young fawn by a doe. Upon Penelope's birth, such a bond almost certainly existed between her and her own mother. Then it was over.

Despite the fact that Penelope could barely walk, her mother chased her away, violently. The instances where Castle ran at Penelope at a gallop, forcing her to flee, were charged with emotion on both sides, the mother harboring a visible rage toward her imperfect offspring. When Penelope was a yearling, Castle could simply have let her be, yet she did not and perhaps could not tolerate her emotionally. At those moments, Penelope fled in fear. When she ran

toward me, she hyperventilated from the exertion of running and from the adrenaline rush of fright, as we have all experienced. Following almost any renewal of her banishment she retreated and withdrew into herself.

As I observe the trust that Carol places in Penelope, it is hard to imagine the consequence should Penelope suddenly abandon her and then reject her outright when she repeatedly tried for a reunion. The trust between them seems inviolable. Penelope calls to Carol, who bleats in return, then runs to her and avidly nurses. They nuzzle each other, lay their heads one upon another, press their faces side by side, simultaneously groom each other, licking necks, heads, faces, backs, and legs, for no evident purpose but the pleasures of touch and oneness. Their loving interaction brings me deep happiness. Penelope has been the most solitary of souls. I wanted her to have someone of her own kind, her own flesh and blood to bond with, to share motion and rest, food and water. I wanted her to experience being the most important thing in the world for Carol, and Carol for her. She has it. She also has me. I do not know my position in the hierarchy of Penelope's world. My relationship with Penelope is not the same as her relationship with Carol, yet increasingly it appears that it is not so different. Seeing me at a distance, Penelope's tail wags and she begins moving directly toward me in the way that Carol wags her tail and moves toward her mother upon sighting. Carol knows that Penelope is the source of her nourishment as Penelope knows that I am the source of hers.

The instant we see each other I am filled with love, and a degree of peace. My simple joy in being with her does not fade or change from day to day or from year to year. It is perhaps an example of love in its truest sense, the love some mothers feel for their offspring through the decades, no matter what transpires. Would I feel these emotions if she had no feeling toward me? I would be capable of caring for her, might even be committed to her care as a means of nurturing another life, one that has been in need and which appears at the door each day to be cared for out of its own self-interest. Although I took care of Penelope's mother, brother, and sister for months, feeding them each day, I did not feel love for them. They did not seem to love me. Penelope comes to me when she is hungry and I feed her, but we interact on a complex of levels simultaneously, and it may be that the largest of these is emotional.

Instinct alone may not explain a progressive connection between a wild animal and a human, nor allow for such connection. Overriding forces may have needed to come into play. As would a man or woman who has been previously hurt or wounded by betrayal or rejection in a romantic relationship, Penelope approached me with caution, but her caution was not physical. For months she would stand inches from me and lower her head, which rendered her vulnerable. The greater risk, the true caution, was evidently emotional, the risk associated with allowing herself to touch me. If I then betrayed her, it would have cut on another level. One year ago this week, when the bond of trust was finally addressed, when Penelope hyperventilated the moment she first took food from my hand, it was the release of emotional withholding.

As day by day she allowed me to care for her, elements of her early experience may have been reflected in our exchanges. Because it was she, again, who, three days after the first physical contact, began to groom me. Penelope does not interact with non-cervine animals. She does not have active relationships with squirrels, birds, or dogs. She does not feed these animals, they do not feed her. She and they do not stroke each other affectionately. Early on, she may have sensed or hoped that I could share this with her, could provide it, as I provided food. That she has developed and practiced interaction with a single human is outside the normal boundaries of a wild deer's experience. Her equipment to approach our connection, her deliberation in judging its qualities, may have been developed and tested through a combination of cognition, intuition, and emotion. She is capable of projecting and weighing possible consequences. She may have carried an overt or buried awareness of her maternal abandonment, as her rejection was reenacted in the months of her solitary existence and continued after her connection with me began. We have a complex bond which both overrides and recognizes limitations because we are of different species. If Penelope saw me as a mother substitute, she also knew that a mother can turn on her, can viciously reject her at her moment of vulnerability, pain, and need, and it would have been understandable for her to mistrust me no matter my actions. Not only must she have been weighing my foreignness as a member of a different species, but also been weighing my individual qualities, my essence apart from specifics, my evident differences from her mother and the ways in which I might not have been different enough.

AUGUST 15

Last night Barbara came over, leading a very young girl by the hand, her niece, Willow, who stood transfixed by the sight of a man touching a deer. For her part, Penelope showed the caution she exhibits with strangers. She knows Barbara, but Willow was new. Penelope stared at the child, looking my way periodically. I gave her assurance, saying "It's okay, no one will hurt you," and making the palms-forward gesture to signify her safety. I wonder whether Willow was the youngest human Penelope had ever seen, and whether new motherhood might be attracting her attention to a person roughly the size of her fawn.

The intense temperature of the past week, with heat index of 110 degrees and one hundred percent humidity, has affected Penelope's broken limb the same way it affects people with bone injuries. She is hobbling so badly that she walks on her left front knee, the entire lower leg unable to support any weight, throwing her body wildly out of alignment. This morning, as it was growing light, I saw her making her way toward me with extreme difficulty.

To save her extra steps, I quickly went to meet her. I gave her an extravagant breakfast, all of it chilled. In addition to her strawberries, grapes and apples, I offered her a fresh peach, something she had never had. I first extended the whole peach for her to examine

I was witnessing the signs and signals conveyed by a wild animal to express the idea of a relationship with a human having its own forward motion. Had I not seen them, I would not have been able to imagine them.

and sniff, then sliced a piece and placed it between her lips. When she receives a novel taste there is a moment as the flavor develops and is considered, then the signs of acceptance, rejection, or approval. She loved her peach, and was greedy for each piece, finishing every scrap and fiber I could find in the crevasses of the pit.

Seeing her hobbling so severely removes any comforting notion that she has recovered from her injury. She does have stronger days, and weaker. I have seen her run on her broken limb under duress, but there has been no mending or straightening, and even with strengthened muscles she is vulnerable to every threat. If Penelope should further injure her bad leg or become immobilized by a second disabled or even temporarily injured limb, if her strength and mobility decline, should she be unable to walk or to care for Carol, I would need to ensure her protection. I could make an open shelter for her, a lean-to or manger, bringing her breakfast and dinner and collecting fresh leaves and grass. I don't know how much indigenous greenery she eats in a day, but she spends many hours finding it. Her meals with me may be a highlight but they are far from all she needs, and if she could not walk I would have to provide.

There is another matter; in the United States it is against the law to "keep" a deer. The government finds and euthanizes tamed deer. Their justifications are incomprehensible to me. People have reported sudden "visits" from state agents with guns and the summary shooting of any deer or fawn that is being kept. But if there were no fences, no ropes, chains or collars, no moats, gates, or enclosures, Penelope would not be kept, she would be free, and on the property because she chose to be.

AUGUST 19

For almost half an hour this morning Penelope licked my hands, my arms, and my face. At the same time, I stroked her, from her muzzle to the base of her spine. I have learned, from watching her with Carol, just how vital the physicality of grooming is. Often, when she licks me, the grooming picks up its rhythm, she enters a trancelike state and she does not want to stop. If, before she gave birth, she used me as a surrogate of sorts, as a stand-in for her absent mother and her unborn fawn, then she was enacting a practice necessary to being a full deer, in the way certain behaviors feel necessary to being a full human. She has had her own fawn for the past three months and she nurses and grooms Carol every day, yet she still wishes to groom me.

Every morning, when Penelope appears, I usually look up to find the fawn following her, strong and healthy, a bit bigger than she was the day before, more solidly present, more confidently positioned in the world. I tell Penelope, "You are such a good mother, the best. You have done beautifully in taking care of your baby. I am so proud

of you." And as the sun comes through the trees, I place fruit between her lips, she presses her face against my torso. It is a celebration of our victory of life over death, and we have another day.

AUGUST 24

At dinnertime last night Penelope was by herself, and at sunrise she arrived alone again. She appeared to have thought Carol would be with me and, not finding her here, grew agitated. Aware of a group of deer on the next property, she walked a few paces in their direction and began to call. When she realized that Carol was not among the others, Penelope's affect shifted. In the same way a human mother, out of touch with her child, might assume the child is with neighborhood friends, then finding otherwise begins to panic, calling the child's name with increasing frequency.

She started wandering in one direction then another, calling intermittently, then calling in a continuous stream. Penelope walked purposefully southward and I went with her. She kept calling to her fawn, looking in every direction, moving quickly, the two of us searching. After a while I went to check the road for any sign, found none, and finally returned home.

Two hours later, through an open window, I heard Penelope's call. "Oh, this is bad," I thought, "she's still looking for Carol."

I went out. Penelope was moving toward me in a straight line, calling and calling, as she had been two hours earlier, but she was not calling to Carol, who was following right behind her. She was once again calling to me, sharing the news, telling me "I found her." I joined them and fed them, celebrating the reunion.

Carol is more independent than most fawns her age and she must have gone off on her own for a while. Maybe she had stayed out all night. The sound of Penelope's call to her lost fawn held the same desperate edge as a mother's cry to a lost child, a measure of what her fawn means to her, the fear of loss profound. The temporary loss of contact, which became temporary only after it was resolved, incited strong anxiety, turning to panic, giving way to relief, all emotions which occur in one who loves another. Penelope knew that I shared her anxiety over Carol's disappearance because I went with her in search. Understanding our shared concern, once Carol was with her, two hours later, Penelope brought her to show me and used her voice to tell me.

AUGUST 25

Attempting to research the vocal sounds a doe uses to call her fawn, every reference I found for 'deer calling" was directed toward the killing of deer: how to lure a doe by mimicking the call of a fawn in distress, for example. If the impersonation is done properly, the mother comes, the hunter kills her. The human might feel that he has outwitted a dumb animal, might feel that the body strapped to the roof of his truck is his rightful trophy, an earned mark of human superiority.

The body on the truck's roof rack, no longer breathing, still exists in the present tense. Miles behind the departing truck there is a fawn left alone who now has no mother, has no one to feed her, nurture, and protect her. The body, which will be butchered, renamed "venison," and cooked, is still loved by its fawn or fawns. The venison might have left behind siblings, and perhaps left behind its own mother, who might go in search, might grieve, scan the woods, sniff the vacant bed, the love between them not having been extinguished by arrows or bullets.

The dead deer held knowledge and memory, had dreams at night, knew its family members, and others, by scent and by sight, had an individual personality, specific likes and fears, possessed a sense of play and perhaps, like Penelope, had a sense of humor. The venison may recently have felt anxiety over a missing fawn, might have called to it, living in hope of being reunited. Hunters debate among themselves how old a fawn should be—the consensus is four months—before they can kill its mother.

Humans are traditionally and perhaps intrinsically carnivorous, and there is specific legitimacy in taking life in order to survive. Taking young life for sport and trophies is another matter. Having worked to attract one individual deer—not with mimicked calls but with kindness, for the purpose of enhancing her survival, prolonging her life, making her happy—the deceptive act of calling to kill, of pretending to be a fawn in order to take the life of a mother, strikes me as alien. I have found my own ways to call to Penelope, greeting her with gently spoken words, speaking her name, making hand gestures, all of which she responds to by approaching, knowing that I will behave consistently, that I do not behave in one way as a means of disguising an intention to behave in another.

Penelope accepts that I understand her spoken language, as she understands some of mine. Whether the deer now consider me half-man half-deer, in this matter I am proudly on their side and do not side with the humans who would do them harm.

AUGUST 30

Yesterday evening I fed Penelope and Carol an extravagant tasting menu of peaches, strawberries, blueberries, red grapes, green grapes, black grapes, champagne grapes, and apples. Carol wanted to try everything. When the feeding was done they stayed, moving about, close to each other, and I thought of all that Penelope has, the golden life she is enjoying.

I told her she was not alone, and she is not alone. I told her I was watching over her and I watch over her. I told her that if she came to me, I would care for her, and she has come, and I care for her.

2017

Fully alive

JANUARY 10

It will soon be two years that Penelope and I have been part of each other's daily lives. She and Carol have lived to see this new year and it is a gift I cannot take for granted. Surviving against odds, none of the usual perils have harmed them. Penelope's evident awareness that she is loved has intensified. She has arrived at a sustained moment, with a home and a small family of her own. She seems also to understand that her privileges have extended to her fawn by birthright.

Apart from her disabled limb, Penelope seems as healthy as any of the other adult deer. She is a diligent and watchful mother, in contrast to the abandonment and neglect she suffered. She has included me in Carol's life, and when the three of us stand together in a close circle, when we are all touching each other at the same moment, it feels that a complex bond of trust has been formed. Carol learned early that I was a source of kindness, of pleasure and nourishment. By observing me with her mother, and by testing me personally, she learned that

Penelope

I would not hurt her. There are mornings when Penelope may have stayed asleep or shown little inclination to stir, and Carol makes her way to the property. On seeing me she wags her tail and approaches. She eats from my hand without her mother's watchful presence, and I now have relationships with each of them. I feel that I can already see signs of Penelope's second pregnancy, which would be two and a half months advanced. She is most likely carrying twins. Having carried a fawn to term, having delivered, protected and nursed her, Penelope will this year be an easier mother, will know what is happening, will know that I am watching, and that I am in her corner.

MAY 20

As she lay in her big leaf bed after breakfast, I sat close to her with coffee and the paper and for two hours we rested companionably in the early light. Penelope is ready to deliver soon and seems rightfully

exhausted. I can see the life inside her, squirming, sometimes kicking. She turns to lay her head against the pulsating bundle inside her and closes her eyes, listening, or focusing on the sensations. She surely knows, this year, what the feelings and motion mean. Her quiet head against her own abdomen is an action of caring for the new fawn or fawns, safe within her, still separated from the outer world by only a thin wall of flesh, muscle, skin, alive together.

In early evening, Penelope came by herself and stood beside me, after what had been a long day. Our moments before sunset are gentle, without the desperation of breaking a long night. She is tired. Her hunger is subdued, understood, almost beside the point. I could see that her leg hurt, as it often does after a day of stress, and now especially with her gravidity. We stood in the last light. We hadn't seen each other in twelve hours. She pressed her face against my skin and I relaxed to the feel of her body, warm and soft. I gave her good apples, grapes, strawberries. Before she could take the last bite of berry she had an urgent moment, one I recognize from last year's pregnancy. She will never relieve herself in front of me and, like a lady, always goes off to a private place. She moved quickly away, toward a wild edge of the property. When she was done, she sank into one of her preferred resting spots, under an oak in the deer sanctuary.

From inside, I kept an eye on her through the window as it grew dark. She is my girl. I want nothing to befall her, no pain or fear or loss, only goodness and love, and seeing her full of new life, I felt the peace of knowing that she was within my range of protection, safe for now.

MAY 24

As of six this morning, Penelope had still not delivered. The past three days she has been relaxed with me and as I feed her, I rest my left palm against her abdomen, feeling the nascent life inside. She seems to enjoy the contact and it is a sign to her that I know what is taking place within her body. She is welcoming me into her pregnancy directly this time, and by touching her in the relevant parts of her body I am sharing in it. In the year since Carol was born, she has seen that I welcome her offspring as I welcome her, and she may reasonably project that her enlarging family will enjoy her privileges.

MAY 25

Penelope settled in the leaf bed last night and as it was getting dark I said goodnight to her and went inside. She was still there at five this morning, barely glimpsed through first light, tone on tone. I want her to be near and was glad she had stayed. The morning was cool, she ate her warm soup eagerly and I marveled at her size. After she finished her breakfast, I placed my hand on her side. There was nothing to distract her from my touch and she did not move away. It is another level of acceptance, a further degree of physical closeness. I am curious to see whether this prenatal touching will have an effect on my bond with the fawns.

An exceptional day

JUNE 4

The question is answered.

In this morning's first light, Penelope came toward me. She stopped and doubled back a few yards. She approached again, followed by a tiny fawn taking its first steps. The unsteady, stiff-legged gait made clear that it had been born within the half hour.

Penelope led the fawn directly to me, stood close while she nursed, then urged the infant's face against my leg. She encouraged me to touch the new life. I bent and very gently stroked the fawn. Once she had established the connection between us, Penelope purposefully walked off, leaving her newborn with me.

She had clearly delivered twins and had brought one to me to care for.

While they were still in the womb, I had named them Iris and Cyrus. The newborn I had just been given was Iris, I decided. At this exquisitely vulnerable moment, Penelope had entrusted her care and protection to me. Having followed her mother here, Iris knew to

Penelope

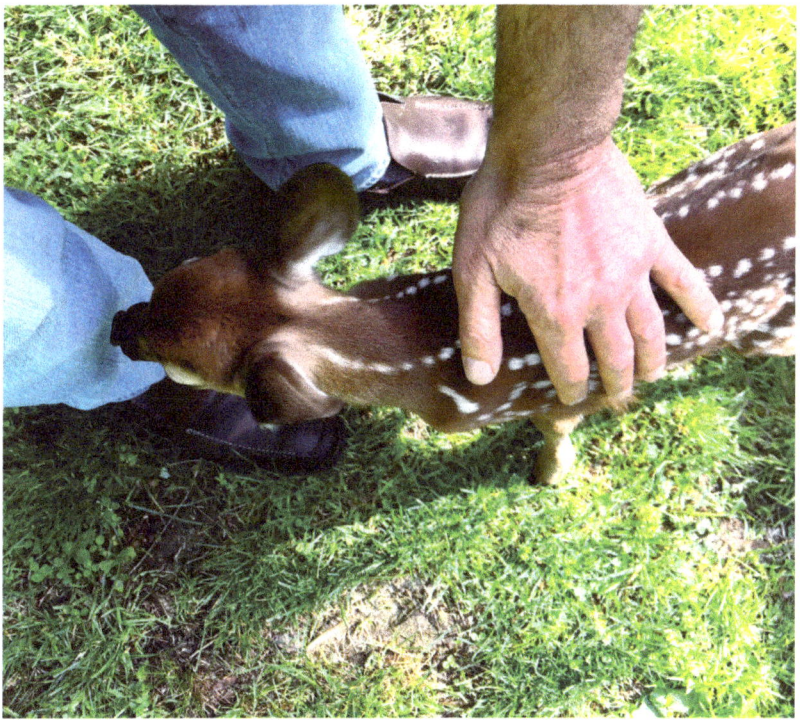

> *If our bond of trust required proof, it was here.*

stay with me and not follow her away. A doe has a specific means of communicating commands to her fawn, by muzzle touch, I believe, and Penelope must have told Cyrus to "wait," told Iris to "come." Once here, she told Iris to "stay, I'll be back." I watched Penelope walk about four hundred feet, flanked by Carol, as she went to care for the other fawn herself. Penelope stopped at the hiding place of the second twin, and I saw her attending to Cyrus in the distant bushes, just where I guessed she had placed him. I could not have expected what was happening. Presented with two new lives, Penelope had chosen one of them as hers, one as mine, knowing that I would understand what she wanted of me.

Iris was at ease with me and seemed to have no anxiety being separated from her mother. She had spent her initial half hour with Penelope—I had witnessed her nursing—so it was not a matter of imprinting on me. At the urging of her mother she was forming a secondary attachment. Iris may have known my hand through the womb, and she had heard my voice, filtered through her mother's body. Penelope's signals told her that I am to be trusted. I was the fourth living thing Iris encountered in her first minutes, after Cyrus, Carol, and her mother.

The morning was gentle and bright, the world at the height of its spring glory. There could not have been a better day for Iris's introduction, the light, the air, the fragrance. In my eyes, she was the most beautiful creature, the perfection of life. She and I stayed together for four hours and she did not leave my side. We moseyed around the yard and at intervals she lay at my feet to have a nap. I stood or crouched beside her while she slept, and when she awoke, I stroked her again as I would a puppy, reveling in the level of comfort and connection between this newly born fawn and myself. She has blue eyes, which I have never seen in a fawn. When Penelope returned, she nursed Iris, the three of us standing as close together as possible.

I can't know whether Penelope had been aware she was carrying twins and had worked out her plan in advance, or whether she was surprised by two new lives emerging, each needing care. Upon giving multiple birth, a doe places twins or triplets separately for their first two weeks, which brings demands on the mother, but unlike most wild deer, Penelope possessed a solution; she could bring one twin to me, knowing that I would do what was needed, leaving her free to care for the other. If our bond of trust required proof, it was here.

JUNE 8

Since the birth, Penelope has been staying near me, sleeping on the property for much of each day, resting against the house, under the bedroom window. Iris has her hiding spot, in a tall cluster of shrubs which I have let grow in anticipation of this purpose, in the deer sanctuary, outside the kitchen windows. She is invisible there, and when Penelope rouses Iris she brings her around the corner into the yard and leaves her with me for three or more hours each day. Penelope then goes to tend to Cyrus, whom I have seen only at a distance. Nursing her twins, Penelope is remarkably hungry and has already asked to be fed four times today, eating roughly twenty pounds of fruit. I give her all she wants and when she has finished, she wanders away to forage for leaves and flowers. At six each evening

she is waiting, starving, having nursed each of her twins several times through the day. Once both fawns have been safely stowed in their places for the night, Penelope lies on the lawn, or in her leaf bed, relaxing in the last of the day's light. In her need for comfort and protection, her feelings of belonging, I sense changes, and we sit in peaceful silence.

Penelope is a tender and attentive mother. Several people have suggested that my loving treatment of her may have provided her with a model of maternal care, countering her early experience.

JUNE 12

Penelope is displaying unmistakable signs of wanting to come into the house.

JUNE 16

This evening Penelope brought both fawns to me. It was my first sighting of the twins together.

She shows exemplary commitment to her fawns. Each is healthy and fine. She knows what is needed for their safety, and for twelve days she has kept them in widely separated hiding spots. Now that they are strong and large enough to emerge and walk as a family, she has allowed them to be together.

The four of us stood close to each other. As if aware that this was a moment of affirmation, Penelope placed them under the red maple and stood behind them, all three facing me. I took a photo. The

Penelope

tree would seem to have significance to Penelope; under its branches is where she first groomed me, and it is where, a year ago, I took a similar photo of her with Carol. She has often napped beneath it, and she may feel it as a room of her own.

Whenever she has contemplated a change that embraces the next level of trust, I have sensed it. Since the birth of her twins, we have reached that new level. For the first time, as I had predicted, Penelope came all the way inside the greenhouse. She appears to have overcome any unease about the interior. She entered, with her entire body inside, I fed her, and when she had eaten all she wanted she backed out. She had tested it, and her freedom and sovereignty remained intact.

JUNE 17

The idea of eating indoors has been settled; this is where she now wants her meals.

JUNE 19

Getting out of the rain today, Penelope entered the greenhouse, and right behind her was Iris.

Only fifteen days old, Iris has already done what took her mother two years of testing. Coming inside was not about me of course, but about following her mother, and following her mother's silent instructions. Iris looked around, took a few steps and went back out. In my budding relationship with this young life, she has accepted my touch from her first half hour, and now at two weeks of age has entered the house.

Watching Penelope nurse her twins, seeing her lick and nuzzle them, and feeling the way she extends that grooming toward me, I sense her fulfillment. This morning in the silence of predawn, no one else awake, we had only each other. I greeted her with green grapes. She pressed her face against my torso, then with her nose and muzzle lowered my hand and the fruit it was holding. When our feeding had concluded she licked my hands and arms. Following her second feeding at seven, she urged me to play, which I now take as a form of recognition and equality and I know to return in proper measure. I stroked her neck and the top of her head, her muzzle and cheeks, her flanks. She held up her broken foot, the rounded wrist extended, and I turned my arm and wrist in a similar way and extended them to her. She rocked toward me in a gentle lunge, and I rocked toward her, in kind.

JUNE 21

Summer solstice.

At four thirty it was already light, and as Penelope was eating her grapes, she became suddenly alert to something she could smell but not immediately see; the distant approach of another deer. Penelope moved toward the deer and I went with her. It was Carol, coming toward her mother with hesitation. I had not seen Carol in almost a week. She has been temporarily banished, the separation nature's method of allowing the new mother to properly care for her newborns. I will be happy when Carol is reunited with her family, which should happen within a month. She knows that I welcome her, even as her mother has warned her off.

Drawing close to Carol, Penelope put her ears back, her head lowered, a warning, moving toward her firstborn with slow aggression before walking straight past her and away. Carol seemed confused; it may be projecting to say she was hurt by it. She was, however, visibly hurt in a more direct way, with a linear wound along her back, parallel to her spine, about fourteen inches long, made by a pointed hoof which razed her fur and broke the skin. From the freshness of her blood, it had clearly happened within the preceding three or four hours. Whoever had inflicted the injury had snuck up on her, probably as she slept. Maybe the pain is why Carol came seeking her mother.

It is hard to think of another deer attacking Carol, especially at this time of isolation. When I beckoned to her she seemed uncertain,

Paul Bochner

Penelope

but she came, taking grapes and apples from my hand, hungry for the contact, bringing her nose and mouth up to my own, making strong eye contact. I want her to know that I will care for her as fully as ever. She may have no way to know that her mother's rejection is temporary, although I am not certain that there is much the deer do not know.

When Carol does rejoin Penelope, the family I envisioned will be real. My hope, when the twins are older and fully mobile, is that the four will travel their range as a herd, with Penelope as the matriarch.

By nine forty Penelope had come for another feeding, her third in five hours. She is chronically starving since the delivery, her udder swollen with the nursing of two growing lives.

JUNE 22

In the late light, near sunset on the longest day of the year, Iris ran and leapt, twisted, scurried, and danced. I fed Penelope for the fourth time of the day, the fragrance of strawberries twined with the honeyed light, suffusing the moment, yet I sensed that she was upset with me, perhaps because my attention was divided between her and her baby's revels. As she was in the middle of being fed strawberries, she took Iris and walked off, not looking back.

Today, after a period of months when she has been here every day and night without fail, beginning in earliest light and continuing into late darkness, she was not here at dawn, not here this morning, not here at noon, and has not come this afternoon.

Yet at four this morning, Carol was waiting, seemingly unsure as to whether I am now changed toward her, as her mother is changed. Uncharacteristically, she would not eat from my hand and every time I extended it she bolted. Emotions are running, in this season of birth and renewal. At seven thirty this evening, in the last light, Penelope was at the door. I fed her several large apples, green grapes, a whole pound of strawberries. When her bowl was empty, I went back and came out with a large bunch of black grapes and fed them to her one by one. Then I gave her another half dozen strawberries. When she had finished those, we sat together on the lawn. After a moment she rose, came up very close, and began to paw at me. I made light of it with a similar half-gesture. She took several serious swipes at me, with her folded front foot. Her eyes showed what I know is her anger. She swiped at me again—if her leg were not disabled she could have torn me deeply with her sharp hoof—then she again stormed off, moving away from me as fast as she could, without hesitation or a parting glance, down the embankment and across the road.

The demands of motherhood are increasing, her growing, nursing fawns must be taking more and more from her body, her hormones may be unbalanced, from pregnancy and birth. She may again be yearning for an end to her chronic pain. She is uncharacteristically angry, and while her mood swings are perhaps unrelated to my actions, her ire is directed toward me.

JUNE 29

Last night Penelope was fully in a foul mood, tired and impatient with her twins. Cyrus kept trying to nurse and she threw him off, stepping over him, wanting only my attention, wanting her dinner, wanting the flies to leave her alone. Following a seven-month pregnancy, she has been nursing her twins for nearly a month. She has been caring for two fawns in two locations, traveling between them several times each day, making sure each is safe, well-fed, and healthy. She has been keeping them clean, gauging the moment when they were ready to emerge and be with her full time, throughout the day. Last night she wanted none of it. I feel that if she could have left them for the evening, come to me on her own, been fed a good dinner, and then sat on the lawn for a nap, as she did while pregnant, she would have. As it was, she seemed upset with me for not managing her situation. And again, she stalked off after eating, headed for the road. Her twins followed her.

An hour later they came back. Penelope may have rested beside the water, taken a dip in the pond, nursed Iris and Cyrus. She was clearly feeling less stressed. I fed her again and they all stayed until it became dark.

JULY 9

Penelope seems worn down, moving with greater than usual difficulty, hobbling badly.

JULY 11

Last evening, light rain began to fall. I was reading in the hammock, Monk lying against my side, dry under the canopy, weightless, a moment of true peace near the day's end. I heard Penelope's voice, the vocal capability which will be gone again as soon as her fawns are weaned. I looked up to see her standing a few feet away, Iris and Cyrus at her side. She was using her voice to let me know she was there, and I acknowledged her by getting up and coming back with her fruit bowl. As I fed her, the twins meandered and foraged together, side by side, Monk resting in the hammock, facing us. The rain tapered, the sun appeared, gilding us all.

JULY 14

Penelope's disability and resulting abandonment might easily have led to her early death. She has lived three years, has been a fine mother to yearling Carol, and is now also mother to twin fawns who are five weeks and five days, strong, safe, and healthy. Although Penelope has shown emotional fragility, and has been irritable, her temperament has also changed in positive ways since the birth of the twins. When she arrives for her feeding, she walks into the house with a sense of fresh pleasure in her mealtimes, and the comfort of our mutual touching. If I needed to sum up Penelope's state of being using only a single word, it would be happiness. Tonight, when she came inside, I fed her the apples she loves; Ambrosia, Smitten, Fuji, gave her green grapes, and black, placed strawberries between her lips. She seemed to savor their fragrance and I sniffed them with her as she took her first bites.

Tonight's dinner appeared to give her even greater than usual pleasure. When she had eaten, she walked out of the greenhouse to her waiting babies. I went with her, the four of us moving slowly on the grass, the day fading in a peaceful moment, Earth and its creatures in harmony. I photographed Penelope with her fawns, the light and color fleeting, as darkness approached. I could not have imagined what was about to happen.

Penelope

When it pivots

JULY 15

Before dawn, the moment I went out, Iris and Cyrus ran to me, conveying a sense of alarm. I looked around. I could not see Penelope in the predawn greyness and felt sure she must be only a few yards away. Iris stood staring fixedly at the doorway, looking past me, as if expecting her mother to appear from inside the house. This told me that they had not seen her since waking, did not know where she was and that they had come to me on their own, hoping that she would be here.

I stroked Iris as I stood with them. For over three hours, we waited together for Penelope, the fawns staying within a few feet of me.

It is noon, Penelope has not shown up. The fawns have stayed close to me, resting, rising, pacing, and calling for their mother.

I drove up and down the road, the length of Penelope's range, and saw no sign of her. I then walked the same length of road, searching inch by inch for hair, blood, tire marks, any clue that Penelope might

have been hit by a car. I walked across the road and through the woods, down to the stream. She has sometimes come to the door without the twins, if she has arisen before they did, but for them to have come without her, for her to be elsewhere, is new and a double alarm signal.

It is two twenty-five in the afternoon. The fawns are still in front of the house. They call for their mother.

Although there would have been no reason for her to have gone to the road in the dark by herself, I called the highway department to ask if there was any record of a deer strike near here, and there was none.

Iris and Cyrus will be six weeks tomorrow. A fawn can survive without its mother's milk at two months of age. I went to buy baby bottles and goat's milk, the closest to a deer's own. I warmed the milk and offered it to each of the twins, without success, but I will keep trying.

The three of us are keeping vigil, eagerly waiting for Penelope's return.

It is eight o'clock in the evening. Penelope has not come. I hear the twins, calling for their mother. They are in the woods across the road where they must have gone in search of her.

It is eight thirty at night. Iris and Cyrus are outside, close to the door, alone.

JULY 18

The twins have staked the property as their home. They know that I am caring for them. Iris refuses the bottle but eats pieces of fruit from my hand, offering kisses afterwards. In the space of a few hours yesterday her comfort in directly taking food grew and now she wants all her fruit from my fingers. Cyrus hovers at a slight distance. I toss small bites to him, which he takes with a wary reserve.

Cyrus calls for his mother, and scans the middle distance, looking and waiting. Iris has stopped her calling. That they do not know where Penelope is tells me that she has not been killed, for if she had been, there would be remains, which they would recognize, by scent and instinct. She has gone away.

This morning, they spotted another pair of twins and a doe. They ran toward the other family and were aggressively rebuffed, first by one of the fawns and then by the mother, and they immediately returned to me. I have observed several times these past days that the distant sight of an adult deer fills them with sudden hope, which is soon deflated.

It would be a violation of their nature to bring them inside, even as it would offer the best means of protection, until their mother returns. They are only six weeks old, but this life is what they know, and the outside world is where they need and want to be. They sleep close to the door and run to me when I appear in the morning, before first light. I have hardly slept, constantly aware that they are without their mother. My dilemma as to how to protect them causes me terrible

unease. I greet them and offer finely cut apples. They seem to intuit the extent of my focus on them. I am not as good as their mother, but they observed my physical connection to Penelope, which may help to confer reflected deer status upon me. The mother-child bond in deer is primary and I can't imagine how the loss will affect them if Penelope does not return. They will lack not only their mother's nutrients but her guidance, neither of which I can provide. Penelope is not here to teach them how to navigate, to caution them about the road and tell them when it is safe to cross. If they could be with me around the clock, I might be better able to protect them, but I don't know the silent signals a mother gives her fawns, the signals to "come with me" and to "stay here until I return," which Penelope clearly imparted to them in their first hours.

Penelope grew up without a mother. Her twins are now motherless at a vitally early age. They have each other, which is a blessing.

JULY 20

Cyrus was outside this morning and spent time with me in the dark. Iris came later. They appear healthy but have not grown as much as they should have. The spirit they exhibited when they were with their mother is dampened. They do not run, leap, or play. They seem numb, and move about slowly, eating vegetation.

At ten this morning, I again went to search for Penelope, clambering down into the woods. The stream runs from north to south, meandering over rocks, the only sound. This is what the deer cross the road for, and it is their own peaceful world, exquisitely verdant and silent. I believe that when Penelope was injured and rejected, she retreated there, to recover or to die. She healed imperfectly, yet enough to restart her life as a solitary soul. Walking through the woods by the stream, hoping for a sign of her, I could feel her early presence.

I made my way through the glen, searching for any glimmer,

Paul Bochner

*I tell myself that
she could re-appear
at any time. Yet
this disappearance
is different.*

finding none. I finally climbed the densely-grown incline, swung over the barrier and walked the third of a mile along the road, home.

JULY 21

This evening will mark one week since Penelope was last seen. The final photograph I took of her gives me pause; I see what I did not sense in the moment. In the fading light, with her body twisted in one direction, her head in another, a stance I had never seen, Penelope is turning away from Cyrus.

When she was seventeen months old, before the birth of her first fawn, when her relationship with me was strongly established, when she and I had our daily pattern of feeding and touching, Penelope vanished. I searched for her and struggled with the possibility that she may have died. Each morning I rose in darkness and sat outside, hoping and waiting. Five weeks later, she reappeared. We resumed with strengthened connection. She had left her range and had, I believe, been south of it during those weeks, perhaps in the company of the Renee herd, which I know to occupy the contiguous range. There is a chance that she has again gone in the same direction, to be with the same deer.

I tell myself that she could reappear at any time. Yet this disappearance is different. She is a mother. This time her leaving, if that is what has happened, may have different roots and is having different results. Since the birth of the twins on June 4 she has been in a volatile state. She has behaved toward me in a range of extreme ways, some unusual, has been close, loving, upset, forgiving, playful, offended, angry.

The long progression of our bond, its testing and measurement, has concerned trust. The past months have been marked by a deepening of that trust, and with it, palpable joy. It has been clear since the birth of her twins that Penelope was exulting in what appeared to be a state of grace. Her body language as she stood at the picnic table in the evening light, watching me approach with her bowl filled with fruit,

was that of a soul who is secure in the knowledge of being wanted, protected, loved. Each aspect of her life was woven into the fabric of contentment and fulfillment. Yet as with every life, her light cast its shadow.

    If I remove her status as a deer and think of Penelope simply as a living being, it more easily becomes clear. I have experienced similar events in relation to other people, those whose early capacity to form human bonds of love and trust has been compromised. When Penelope was only a few weeks old she had an attachment disorder forced upon her, there is nothing else to call it; her development of emotional bonding was disturbed. It is something I understand, perhaps a challenge that we share. In my relationship with her, that disruption has never been far from us, no matter how she and I were developing our own bond. Even as the aspects of trust advanced, they were weighed daily.

JULY 29

Iris and Cyrus have survived two weeks without their mother's protection and without her milk. They have each other, they have me, and several times a day I feed them from my palm, blueberries, grapes, apples, all cut into small bites. They have their sleeping spot, just outside the door, under the swing, as if its suspended surface provides them some form of roof.

I leave the back door open at all times, and if they need or want greater shelter they can enter and sleep inside, coming and going as they wish. They choose to be out. I know I could ensure their literal safety by putting collars and leashes on them, but I cannot do that, cannot violate their essential nature and their physical freedom of movement. I would do so in only the most dire circumstances—an approaching hurricane, a pack of coyotes or other dangerous animals prowling the yard. For any lesser reason it would be wrong. I will try to protect and nurture them while honoring their wildness. At night, knowing they are outside alone, even though they are only a few feet from the door, I can barely sleep, feel strong anxiety, and am greatly relieved to see them before the first light of dawn.

They sleep close to the door and run to me when I appear in the morning, before first light. I have hardly slept, constantly aware that they are without their mother.

Last week, Cyrus disappeared for three days. Iris spent those days lying unusually still, waiting, and she and I each seemed to know that Cyrus had gone on a mission. I don't know how I knew that he had not been hurt, yet I felt no anxiety and knew he would return. Two months old, being the boy, the larger and more independent, the big brother, he went, I believe, to look for their mother. He must have given Iris the signal to stay here and wait, as Penelope had given them such signals when they were younger. When he reappeared after three days, he immediately touched noses with his sister, conveying to her whatever he needed to—"I tried. I failed to find her. It is just us."

JULY 31

Some time ago, I wondered whether her early identity as an isolate might eventually cause Penelope to leave me, to resume her solitary life. Perhaps that is what has happened. Perhaps with the pain and stresses of her disability she felt unequal to the demands of caring for twins. It has been sixteen days since she vanished in the night.

Iris and Cyrus seem physically healthy, having turned eight weeks old yesterday, and they are almost always together. It is Iris who most needs my closeness and companionship. She walks through the open door and into the house, coming to me four or five times each day, whereas Cyrus shows up less frequently. Iris eats pieces of fruit from my fingers with a gentleness I have never experienced in another living being, like feeding a butterfly, the silent, weightless touch of her lips and tongue. She knows the sight of the wooden fruit bowl and she noses around in it for what she wants the most, and I give it to her.

Iris was taught to come into the house by Penelope, who also showed her how to eat from my hand. I strongly feel Penelope's echoing presence in her. Attempting to put together the circumstances of her disappearance, I searched diligently for any sign that she might have been killed in the night. I have determined that she was not killed by a car. If a coyote had ambushed her while she slept with her fawns, I might have heard the commotion. If it happened at all there would be clear signs, her body would be nearby, and I would have found it. The smell would be inescapable, pervasive for weeks, and there would be vultures. Had Penelope been attacked and killed, what of Iris and Cyrus? Imagine that, on their strong legs, they were able to run. They would have returned to the site of their dead mother. They would have known where she was. Had they then come to the door before dawn, it would have been with a very different sense. They would not have been looking past me, as they did, to see if Penelope was in the house.

I believe that Penelope is alive. I believe that internal forces drew her away. I think she knew that her leaving was an incident waiting to happen. She established a connection between me and her fawns strongly and quickly upon their birth, as if needing to know she could rely on my caring for them after she went.

AUGUST 1

Yesterday morning, Leigh, Barbara's and Frank's daughter, called to me from across the lawn and hurriedly told me that a fawn had been hit, a slight distance along the road. I ran down and looking south I saw the splayed and flattened corpse, every limb broken, ripped open to reveal viscera. The accident had happened not many minutes before. On the embankment above, Iris stood looking at the dead body, and looking at me. I gestured toward her with both palms and told her to stay where she was. She watched the scene as a child would, knowing something was wrong, not knowing what she should do, seeming to accept that I would know.

> *I believe that internal forces drew her away. I think she knew that her leaving was an incident waiting to happen.*

Instinct told me that it was Cyrus. There was much damage to the dead fawn, and not enough intact body to move, yet the fawn's fur was largely undisturbed, and I took a photo, to have a way to compare the spots for identification. I moved toward Iris. Six feet above me, she ran along in tandem, toward home. She sprinted the last few yards as I turned up and onto the property and she quickly followed me. She and Cyrus had probably been crossing the road together. Iris had probably witnessed the impact. Staring at the body when I arrived, as if she had been waiting for me, she conveyed that it was her brother.

Iris lay down in a patch of tall grass. I got some apple pieces for her. She would not touch them. I sat beside her for an hour. She was very still, not looking at me, as she usually does when resting, instead turned inward, staring away. In the shade, I carefully studied the photo of the dead fawn and compared it to recent photos of Cyrus. The spots matched.

Iris is nine weeks old. In a span of seventeen days, she has lost her mother and her brother. She had shared the womb with Cyrus for seven months. They had entered the world together, had nursed together, experienced the loss of their mother together and since then they had stayed at each other's sides. I can't say what Iris knew or sensed but I believe she experienced her brother's death. Except for me, she is alone.

Iris eventually rose. I fed her and she walked off, to return a couple of hours later. I fed her four times in the aftermath of the accident. The door to the greenhouse was left fully open for her in case she wanted to be inside, but she slept a few feet from the door, under the swing.

Awakening at three, my instantaneous thought was of Iris, alone in the night. I made coffee and waited. She awoke before five, slowly approaching in the dark, a silent shadow. Were it not for her white spots she would have been invisible, but I sensed her presence. She came toward me and walked straight into the house. I fed her from my hand.

Penelope

    I am not her mother, but maybe I can sustain her. The other fawns her age play and run with their own siblings and they will continue to nurse for the next two months. When Iris and Cyrus were born, I looked upon their ease and grace, feeling the disparity between their early lives and their mother's. In their first six weeks they were in paradise, protected, fed and watched over, by their mother and by me. I thought of how blessed they were, and how remarkable that Penelope, who had grown up alone, who had been brutally rejected by her own mother, could provide them such safety and joy.

    Iris's life has been dealt two losses. She is not injured or in physical pain, and her mother carefully established the bond between us, providing a foster parent for her, something that Penelope did not have at the same age, yet Iris has suffered drastic upheaval. I am certain that Penelope was planning to leave her fawns with me. When she was pregnant with twins, she may have anticipated that she could not properly function as their mother. From the morning of their birth she began to prepare the transition, knowing that I would care for them, that this property would be their home. Penelope gave Iris to me in the first hour of her life. Perhaps she gave us to each other.

AUGUST 10

I have never been so tired, have barely slept. Wanting to be present when Iris needs me, I leave the back door perpetually open and she comes inside many times a day. I keep the wooden fruit bowl filled with the things she likes, rising at three, taking blueberries and grapes from the fridge an hour before I expect her in the morning, so they will be at a moderate temperature. She appears when she wishes and I am delighted to find her standing silently in the greenhouse, looking for me in the kitchen, waiting for me to notice her. I go to her immediately and she eats from my hand. She tells me specifically what she desires at any given moment, appraising the fruit in my palm, selecting what she most enjoys.

Iris is fragile and delicate. She has not grown significantly in the weeks since her mother left and is perhaps a third smaller than the other fawns her age. Her blue eyes have settled into a greenish amber and they are large in her tiny face, her white spots vivid against her tawny coat. She forages, consuming grass, clover, leaves, and flowers, and she comes to me for her fruit. She was deprived of her mother's milk at much too early a moment, something I cannot compensate for. The warm goat's milk I offered from baby bottles was rejected. She is not thriving.

At sunset, Iris cries for her mother. Some evenings she watches the other twins nursing from their own mother, and she moves directly toward them, perhaps hoping to be included, yearning to be nursed as well. The doe and fawns ignore her, and she returns to me.

When Iris cries to be nursed, looking desperately for her mother, I go to her, kneel beside her, stroking her fur and speaking gently. I would give whatever I could, to offer her the comfort she wants, but I cannot give her what she needs, and her cries tear at me.

Carol had not been here in weeks. Feeling that she might offer her little sister something close to mothering, I sent a silent signal into the ether, asking her "Please come and help, I need you."

The next morning, she appeared. I have no way to explain how it happened.

Carol is here and I have succeeded in uniting her with Iris and I am grateful. Carol provides a comforting companionship Iris desperately needs, an adult female, and Iris is visibly basking in the presence of her older sister, something they both clearly enjoy. To reinforce the bond, as I fed them together this morning, I took care to let Carol see the way Iris eats from my hand. Carol knows this is a privilege related to her mother, that only Penelope and her family get fed in this way. I also showed Iris that Carol is fed by hand in the same way she is.

After they had finished their fruit, Carol nuzzled Iris and began to groom her, the first adult grooming Iris had received since her mother left her. She luxuriated in it as Carol licked her head, face, neck, and back and continued for a long while. Iris reciprocated and it became a session of mutual grooming. Iris does not try to nurse from Carol, who is only a yearling, does not have a fawn, and so is not lactating, yet in other ways she has taken her as a surrogate.

Carol now comes to the house each morning at six to be with her sister. When Iris sees her she runs to her, and they have breakfast inches apart, Carol eating from my left hand while Iris eats from my right. When still a fawn, Carol ate in tandem with Penelope and now eats with Iris in the same way. Seeing the tenderness between them relieves some of my stress. By scent or other means, the two sense

Paul Bochner

their kinship, and of course Carol was present the morning of Iris's birth. Each sees that the other is loved.

After grooming, they stroll about the yard in tandem and in these moments Iris seems much less an orphan. At the end of an hour or two, Carol leaves the property, heading south again, and Iris follows her. I always hope that they will spend the day together, yet after a few minutes of walking behind her older sister, Iris returns to the house. I don't know whether she needs the safety of being close to me, whether she may be obeying the instruction her mother gave, to remain here, or both, as Iris stays very near. The door is continuously open, and she freely comes inside and leaves again as she wishes. Sometimes I look up and see Iris standing in the greenhouse, silently, expectantly. I immediately go to her with fruit, and she is always hungry. She presses her head to my legs, standing with her minuscule feet on my shoes, as close as possible, looking up into my eyes. In hers, I see a haunted, hollowed desperation which increases the longer she is without her mother. Under her eyes is a fold of skin which was not there, and which the other fawns do not have. She seems to have stopped growing.

At night she sleeps close to the door, under the swing, where she and Cyrus slept after Penelope left, five weeks ago. It is almost three weeks since Cyrus died. Iris wanders off the property but does not go far before returning.

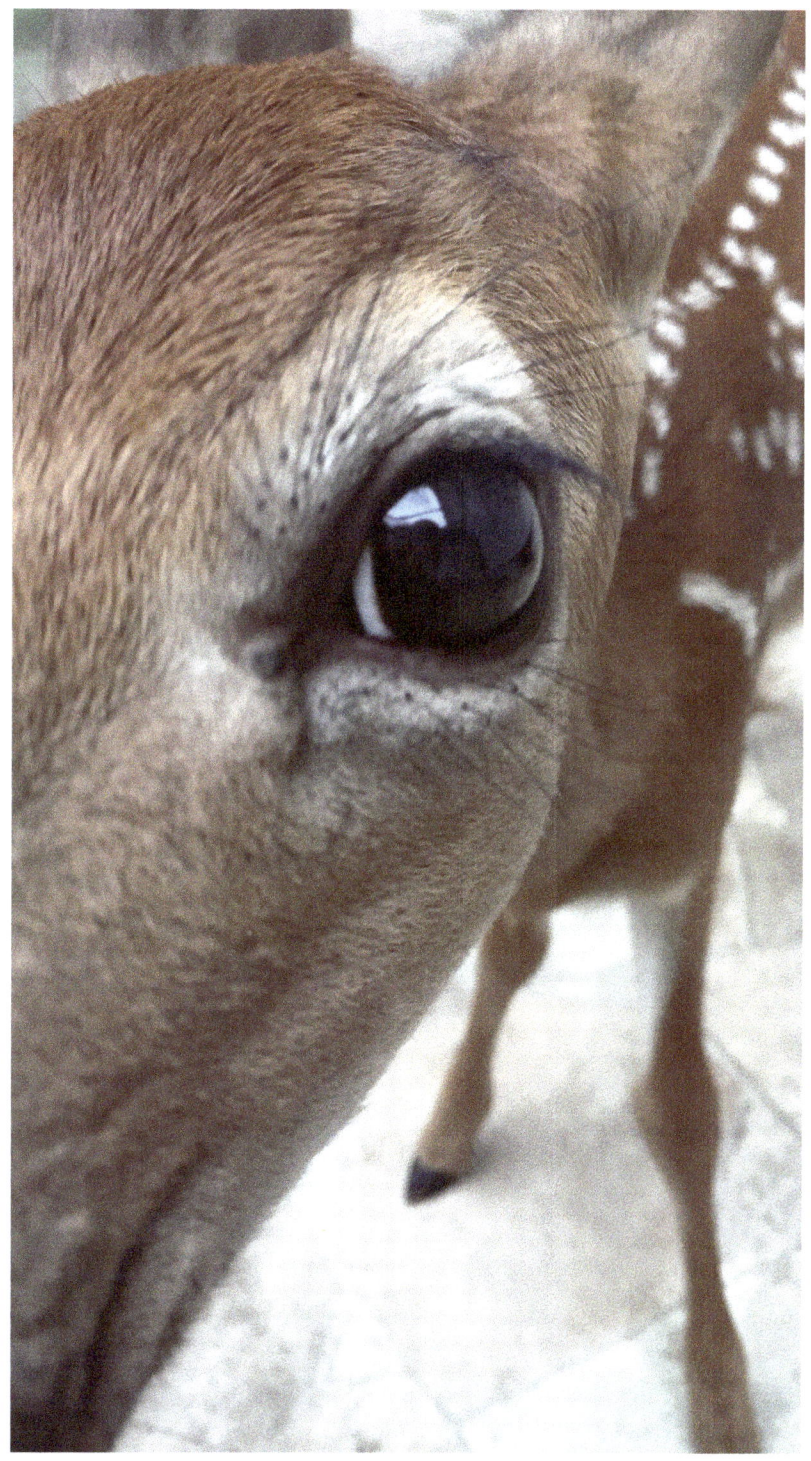

AUGUST 18

It is raining very hard tonight. Iris keeps coming into the house, staying a few minutes, and going out again into the intense darkness and downpour. She is drenched and I wish she would settle, lie down for the night, inside, where I can be sure of her safety. Every time she comes in, I give her a handful of grapes and blueberries, crouching to her level. We hear the rain pounding on the glass roof. If Penelope were here, Iris would nestle beside her and sleep. She needs her mother and her brother, nothing can compensate, yet as she emerges from the rain, back into the house, restless for what she craves and what is gone, she finds me, a respite, and for a few moments we are together. As I watch her, Iris wanders out into the darkness.

AUGUST 19

By morning, the rain had stopped. Before five, as I waited for Iris, a pair of foxes darted back and forth along the edge of the property, down the embankment to the road and back up. I went to the road; there was the smell of death, entrails, a small stomach filled with grass, nothing more. I stared at this last remnant of a life.

On the embankment, Carol stood looking at the road, and at me. It was the same way Iris looked at me as I examined the body of her brother.

I slowly went to Carol and very quietly said, "Come, I'll give you breakfast."

She did not come with me. She turned and walked away. Carol understands more of life and death than I do. She knew that this was the end.

It is noon, I have searched the road on both sides, and there are no further signs. There are no bones or fur. If Iris was hit by a car in last night's dark rain, perhaps her body has been collected, perhaps the foxes dragged away her remains.

AUGUST 20

In the flux of denial and acceptance, part of me holds out a small hope that it was not Iris, that she is elsewhere. I know that she is dead.

I can hardly move, can barely walk, grief accumulating like lead in my limbs, slowing every response, separating soul from body. The phrase "heavy with grief" is real. I know it now, for the first time.

I have lost many, in many ways. I have never been struck so hard by loss. I have never experienced grief like this.

———————

Paul Bochner

Eclipse

AUGUST 21

A rare total solar eclipse is in progress, the first of its kind in a century.

I walk outside and stand in the yard, where so much life has flowed. The dim sunlight is like strange music growing increasingly out of tune. The sun seems to have ceased its shining, and I wonder whether the release from order might extend, impossible things becoming reasonable. In this negation of accepted progressions, the dead and the missing could return.

As dusk approaches at noon, we could stand, in a moment neither light nor dark, celebrating and giving thanks. I will ask Penelope to accept her children again, tell her how I have cared for them. "I told them you would return, told them, 'Soon, your mother will be here, just wait.' They were waiting for you, holding out and holding on as long as they could, even if not long enough. But the eclipse has come, and they have seized this brief chance to emerge from death to be with you."

I will ask her to stay, to never again leave, to allow me to care for them all, to feed them each day, as much as they desire. I stand in the half dark, in the shadows, feeling the eclipse as an open door, and I look for them, seeing those who are not here.

AUGUST 22

The relationship I had built over two and a half years with Penelope was embodied by Iris. My love for Iris is also the love which was mine and Penelope's. Iris lived for eleven weeks. At six weeks she lost her mother, at eight weeks she lost her twin. In a brief span I lost her, and her brother, and her mother. It is not only grief which accumulates in our cells, but everything.

AUGUST 24

It has been six days since Iris was killed. The meaning of six days is unclear. Each morning in darkness I still rise to be ready to greet her and provide the first fruit of her day. The back door remains open. I look into the greenhouse frequently. I expect to see Iris's white spots, and for an instant can almost see them. For the past weeks, when she was alone, at the sight of her I dropped what I was doing and attended to her needs. This is not easily put behind me.

SEPTEMBER 1

The sequence of loss gathers mass and begins to settle. It is two weeks since Iris has been gone. The back door is still open. To close it would be to accept that she has died.

Although I know she cannot come back, I am unable to close the door. It is open for Penelope as well because I believe she is alive, and I live in hope that she will return. My hope and belief that Penelope is alive are grounded in reason. My inability to accept that Iris has died is a new experience. She was so young, and given into

The sound of her cry, calling at dusk for her missing mother, does not leave me.

my care, and whether I failed or whether there was nothing I could have done to save her, the loss is central. Yesterday the vacancy was so hard I wanted to go wherever Iris has gone, to be with her and feed her and watch over her. I wanted to leave behind the human world to care for Penelope's fawn, whose direct connection to life, whose singular purity of spirit and body mean as much to me and are of as great a value as anything else I know. From birth, she was Penelope's gift to me. The days she was in my care were a time of weightless tenderness. My joy in seeing her at three in the morning, at dusk, at any surprising moment she chose to appear, was absolute. Even now I conjure her small pointed hooves, her lips and tongue on my palm, and for an instant she is with me. The sound of her cry, calling at dusk for her missing mother, does not leave me.

SEPTEMBER 3

After two and a half years of daily connection, when almost every aspect of my own life, every need and requirement was placed second to hers, Penelope left.

During those thousand days, from our first contact, she and I each approached the boundaries which separated us and we allowed them to dissolve. At dawn and dusk, under the trees, we both knew that we had crossed a threshold. At the end, few if any barriers were left.

SEPTEMBER 26

At night, I go to Penelope in the dark and quiet, feel her lying alone in the woods, her head against her body and her damaged leg tucked underneath. I see that she is safe, and I place myself beside her.

I feel a tangible line connecting us, attenuated, yet still present. Through it, I know she is alive. I can touch her in this way almost as palpably as I touched her in our final days together, stroking her fur. In the darkness I let her know that the love has not left me and will never leave, that she is missed and wanted.

I think of her leaving, its shape and its details. She has been gone for over nine weeks. Her sense of time, which she showed me encompassed past and present, requires that I carefully consider her sense of future. I increasingly believe that she knew she would leave her fawns, and leave me, that from the birth of her twins she was planning her departure.

Accepting this, much is explained; the increased closeness in our relationship, prior to and immediately following the fawns' delivery, the deepened trust and ease, may all be seen as having been put in place for the purpose of creating a bond, so that the fawns would be with me, so that Penelope could know I would care for them. She may have known instinctively that at two months a fawn can survive without nursing, and she left them one day before they turned six weeks. She could have learned from Carol last year that her fawns would choose to nurse for four months; maybe she knew that my offerings, coupled with the vegetation all around us, would be enough to sustain them.

From the initial days of our connection, in our first months, Penelope had tested me, measuring and weighing my fitness. In our last months she tested my rightness to be her surrogate. She observed my knowledge of the fawns' fragility, the degree to which I welcomed them as her family. From the moment I realized she had gone, I devoted myself to protecting and nurturing them, taking them as my own. She had placed a demand upon me and I accepted it without a thought, respecting their needs and their nature.

I have tried to place myself within her, to experience the moment, in the dark, she walked away from her sleeping fawns and kept walking. I try to imagine what it was like to know, days or weeks before the fact, that she was going to leave the home and the life she had gained, to leave her own offspring, to awaken and know that the hour had come, that tonight was the night, to see in the darkness that her fawns were asleep, that they would not follow her. What was it like to rise, choose a direction, begin walking and not weaken, not hesitate, not stop and turn back? There had to have been resolve. A range of feelings had led her to the moment. It happens in just this way with people who leave home and family in the night, mothers who leave their children.

And to place myself within her feelings and her thoughts, I realize that the larger fact of walking away had been part of her life, almost from its inception, whether Castle had walked away from Penelope in the dark while she slept or whether Castle forced Penelope to walk away, just as she would continue for years to force her to run in fear, the process of leaving was not foreign. She knew, emotionally and cognitively, that such things happen. Yet for many reasons, I do not feel that she abandoned her fawns as her mother abandoned her, don't feel she left me. Any of her actions are validated by a trust that is not undone. Within the broad range of expression she had shared with me, I had observed in her, only once, a moment that appeared to be shame, among the most subtle of emotions, but the glimpse was enough for me to know that she could feel it, and to imagine that, having left her offspring, she might later have wanted to return but felt she could not.

As the weeks passed, I cherished a dream of reunion, imagined seeing her approach one morning in the half-light, her uneven gait, coming toward me. I would be outside, feeding the twins, Carol would be with us. In that moment Penelope would see her family safely together. The twins would run to her in an overflow of exultation, the instant of reconnection they had dreamed of as well, and she would accept them back with a peaceful heart. She would see that I understood much of what she felt, that I knew what she needed, that I had fulfilled the responsibilities she had given me. She would see that her fawns were healthy and fine and would know that her faith in me was not misplaced. Each day that she was gone I had visualized the moment.

After the deaths of both twins, the dream changed. I hoped that when she returned, she could forgive me for having failed.

I had never expected to share a bond of the spirit with a wild animal. It is one of Penelope's gifts to me. There are others I do not understand yet, and it may be years before I am able to name them, even as their value is held close. I attained the privilege of seeing another life fully. In the quiet, under the leaves, we approached each other openly, until we were not a deer and a man but two souls, exultant to be alive, blessed with uncommon love.

Postscript

MAY 22

Last night Carol was waiting at the door. She had walked away the morning Iris died and had been gone almost two years. We stood together under the trees, our ease and comfort still present, as if no time had passed. I spoke to her gently as I fed her. She has suffered a compound fracture, an injury eerily similar to her mother's. It seems to have happened recently, one of the bones in her lower rear right leg is protruding and bloody, and she is surely in pain. I can't imagine the effort it cost Carol to make the journey back here with one broken leg, yet she came.

Early this morning, in the emerging light, I looked through the front windows and watched as Carol gave birth. She had returned to deliver her fawn where she herself had been born, where Penelope was born, in the exact spot in the deer sanctuary where so many have been delivered. The newborn is Penelope's progeny, life continuing, flowing from her own saved life.

Carol had held an image, a memory of this property, where she had been protected and nourished. Wherever she has been, she has clearly had a place where she has been living these past two years, from which she emerged when I silently asked her to come help me with Iris, and where she returned after Iris died. It is probably in the forested mountains, several miles to the south.

It is unusual for a doe to have left her natal range, and I feel there are not many things which could have led her to do so. Everything the deer have taught me suggests a simple reason for Carol having gone, and for having stayed away all this time. She has been with her mother. If that is true, it offers me hope that as Carol came back when she was ready, so, in her own time, Penelope may come home.

As I welcomed her on that first night, years ago, I will welcome her with an open heart, to begin again.

2025

Her descendants know that this is their home.

Acknowledgments

I am increasingly grateful for the many good people in my life, who are simultaneously present within the spectrum of time.

A primary debt of gratitude is owed to Hendrik Hertzberg, at the New Yorker, who first considered me a writer when I was identifiably a painter.

More directly, I am most thankful to Manuela Hoelterhoff, whose gift for shepherding others is well known. Being told one evening of an unusual relationship developing between a deer and myself, she said, "It's a book. You have to do it."

I am grateful to Anne Serling, whose generous reading and instincts for sharing led to Chris Johnson. Chris's open-hearted response and impulse toward connection led to Robert Mrazek.

I owe more than simple thanks to Bob, and will go on thanking him over time, for his gently guiding hand and hard-won wisdom. Working with him, and with Tom Hurd, who has a subtle eye and seems able to do almost everything, and the others on their team, has been a pleasure.

My thanks to Gene Stone for setting aside his work to read the manuscript straight through, and for putting himself on the line to help it into the larger world. I thank dear friend and bright spirit Polly King for reading it and sending it to Gene, and, less strangely that it might seem, I actually get to join illustrious company in thanking Maxwell Perkins - this is true - because without him there would be no Polly. In the same spirit, I am allowed to thank Rod Serling, who knew so much about time's fluidity, and without whom there would be no Anne, whose book about her father led us to connect, and on it goes, moments and years holding much mystery. And I thank John Schneider for his own timing and microtonally-tempered ear, finding the exact note.

My sincere thanks to Madeline Mafilios for her original design concepts and exceptionally fine focus.

www.ingramcontent.com/pod-product-compliance
Lightning Source LLC
Chambersburg PA
CBHW061252230426
43665CB00026B/2914